CULTURE HACKS

26 IDEAS TO **TRANSFORM** THE WAY YOU **WORK**

COLIN D. ELLIS

This book is dedicated to my Uncle Brian,
who tragically died of the COVID-19 virus
as I started to write it.

His stories would have filled ten books
and had you laughing for weeks on end.

'A good laugh is sunshine in the house.'
– William Makepeace Thackeray

Dear Gary

Make positive and productive
workplace culture a reality!

First published in 2021 by Major Street Publishing Pty Ltd
E | info@majorstreet.com.au
W | majorstreet.com.au
M | +61 421 707 983

 A catalogue record for this
book is available from the
National Library of Australia

ISBN: 978-0-6487963-4-3

Cover design by Tess McCabe
Author photograph by Melissa Martin
Internal design by Production Works
Printed in Australia by Ovato, an Accredited ISO AS/NZS 14001:2004
Environmental Management System Printer.

10 9 8 7 6 5 4 3 2 1

CONTENTS

Introduction **1**

Business as usual… but better **7**

How to use this book **11**

Culture Hack #1: Reduce your email **13**

Culture Hack #2: Make time for teamwork **21**

Culture Hack #3: Plan in procrastination **29**

Culture Hack #4: Transform your meetings **37**

Culture Hack #5: Go on a field trip **45**

Culture Hack #6: Be honest, always **51**

Culture Hack #7: Manage stakeholders uniquely **58**

Culture Hack #8: Induct and onboard to impress **66**

Culture Hack #9: Fail visibly **73**

Culture Hack #10: Create a book group **80**

Culture Hack #11: Hold a hobby expo **87**

Culture Hack #12: Stretch for (postural) success **95**

Culture Hack #13: Bust your bureaucracy **103**

Culture Hack #14: Break out the board games **111**

Culture Hack #15: Start a podcast **118**

Culture Hack #16: Hold a showcase **125**

Culture Hack #17: Write a white paper **133**

Culture Hack #18: Chat with the chief **140**

Culture Hack #19: Go to the movies **148**

Culture Hack #20: Hold an Airbnb offsite **155**

Culture Hack #21: Volunteer as a group **163**

Culture Hack #22: Leave the laptop at work **171**

Culture Hack #23: Job swap **179**

Culture Hack #24: Record a culture video **187**

Culture Hack #25: Hold an interdepartmental sports day **194**

Culture Hack #26: Create a culture club **202**

Thanks **208**

About the author **210**

Soundtrack **212**

Endnotes **215**

Index **225**

INTRODUCTION

We should start with the basics – all the best books do. They don't assume that you have all the answers or that you have one fixed view of something. And when it comes to workplace culture, it feels like there are a million views, all of which continually collide, making little sense – so changing said culture is put in the 'too hard' basket.

To fix something, you have to understand it first.

My son came to me one day and said that his stomach hurt. I was filled with love and empathy, and I sent him to the sofa with a comic book and made him a peppermint tea. After I delivered it to him, he showed me a scratch on his stomach where he'd walked into his desk.

I'd delivered a cure for a problem I didn't understand.

This is what generally happens when people deal with workplace culture issues. The solutions are often things like:

- implementing the latest management method
- switching to open-plan offices
- restructuring
- providing technical training courses
- process redesign

- building an innovation hub
- offering new collaboration tools, and
- implementing new policies.

However, the root causes of the issues are actually things like:

- poor behaviour
- poor performance
- unclear strategy, and
- needless bureaucracy.

As you can see, none of the solutions address the root causes. As a result, organisations tend to give up on change and go back to the command-and-control method while they wait for the next management system to come around in five years' time.

So, what is culture? Culture is the sum of everyone's attitudes, behaviours, skills, traditions, stories and beliefs. Everyone's. Culture doesn't belong to the senior executive team (although their actions have the power to destroy it) or to the People and Culture department (although it's generally the custodian of it).

If the new finance manager loses his temper on day one, it affects the culture. If the warehouse team wins an award, it affects the culture. If the members of the sales team are laughing while they work, it affects the culture, as does the IT team not answering your phone call.

The issue with culture is that most people want to change it, yet don't believe that it's within their power to do so. I recognised this when I was 27. I don't remember the day, but I do remember the job I was doing (I was a project manager for a newspaper group) and what my then boss told me. He said, 'This is the team that you have. It's up to you to make sure that you co-create something where everyone can work well together to hit the targets we have. If you don't, we'll fail'.

I remember feeling a sense of responsibility that I'd never had before. And so, as a highly extroverted individual, I did what anyone with my personality would do – I took the team to the pub. It was a team of introverts. That went well.

Two weeks later, I sat down with my boss and had a bit of a whinge. 'These guys are idiots. They don't want to do anything that I suggest. They just sit there quietly.'

My boss looked at me and asked, 'What have you done differently to engage with them, to create a sense of shared purpose and commitment to what we have to do?'

I told him, 'I took them to the pub twice, and suggested we go go-karting'.

His response was short. 'Maybe – just maybe – you're the idiot?' He said it in a good-natured way (although obviously I disagreed), and then set about explaining what it meant to create a good team culture. These little nuggets of information have served me well for the best part of 20 years, and I continue to share them in the workshops I run with organisations around the world – who are desperate to do what I wanted to do 20 years ago. I've since added a number of other recommendations to the initial advice that I received from my boss, based on my own experience and how the world of work has evolved:

- Get to know each other's personalities.

- Have a vision or purpose that you all believe in.

- Share ideas on what's worked well – from a team perspective – in your previous roles.

- Agree on how you'll work together – when you'll meet and when you'll leave each other alone.

- Make time for some creative thinking.

- Make it okay to disagree – but never agree to disagree, because nothing gets resolved that way.

- Never fall out with each other in public.

- Make fun a priority, but recognise that everyone's idea of fun is different and that the balance always has to be in favour of productive work.

- Mix socially, because that's where relationships and shared stories are created.

- Don't blindly follow the paths of others. Create your own path and invite other people to follow you.

Across my 30-year career as a permanent employee, but especially in the last 20 years, I made the last point my goal. Whenever I started a new job, I brought something different, something new, something that challenged the status quo – and I don't just mean my humour or sense of style (although they helped!). I brought different ways of challenging the bad habits people had fallen into, and of building morale and ultimately the culture of the team so that other people became desperate to join us. We liked working with each other, we had lots of laughs, but crucially, we got the job done.

In one of the last permanent jobs that I held as a senior executive, I had a goal to change the perception, within the business, of the team that I managed. In my third week in the role, I brought the team together and provided them with the feedback I'd been given from others across the business – which, to my surprise, they hadn't heard before.

We then set about creating a team culture that would fix the root causes of this perception. We didn't buy endless solutions, but we did invest in independent facilitation so that we could have honest conversations about what we needed to do differently and how we'd hold ourselves accountable. It took two days, and in seven months we'd changed our stakeholders' perceptions of us.

We did it by getting just 5 per cent better every month.

We didn't need to change everything – there was lots that we did well – so we focused on small things that became 'the way that we do things around here'. In other words: evolution, not revolution.

I covered the mechanics of building culture in my book *Culture Fix: How to create a great place to work*; this book builds on those basics to provide you with 26 ideas to help you become 5 per cent better as a team every month.

You can do them all: I have with my teams. There's nothing here that I haven't done or that hasn't worked well – I've left that stuff out (including the exercise where we'd give everyone a nickname!). But you should still ask yourself, 'Can this work for me within my context and my team right now?' Use your common sense.

As there are 26 Culture Hacks in total, you and your teams can try a different one every two weeks for a year. Alternatively, you could pick one thing every month, or you could divide them across different areas within your team so that different people are doing different things. Or you could put them all in a hat and pick one out to try. You decide! Just do something different. It will make the team memorable in a host of great ways and create stories that you'll share for years.

While I love my current job of public speaking and facilitating corporate workshops to help others co-create great cultures, I do miss the buzz of being part of a team that wants to create something unique. You still have this opportunity – don't waste it.

Colin
Melbourne, Australia, November 2020

BUSINESS AS USUAL...
BUT BETTER

The COVID-19 crisis began two weeks before I sat down to write this book, and almost overnight, organisational culture changed. Those who had taken the time to define their culture and were continually taking steps to refine what they did and remain vibrant, flourished. Their people were able to seamlessly transition to working remotely in distributed teams, and some businesses were able to pivot to produce different outputs and maintain profitability or service levels.

For everyone else, there was a sudden realisation that things weren't going to be easy. As Ed Catmull said in his book *Creativity, Inc.*, 'There's nothing like a crisis, though, to bring what ails a company to the surface'. I'd like to think that, since those early days of the virus in March 2020 and the subsequent isolation, senior managers have realised just how important it is to spend time and money helping staff to define the culture that they need in order to meet their targets.

Like I said, 'I'd like to think that'; however, culture has always played second fiddle to, well, everything really. As restrictions started to be lifted, organisations rushed to remove development budgets that would have allowed managers to invest in the very things that would safeguard the organisation from this kind of event in the future. 'Culture's the most important thing' – until it's not, of course. More time and money gets spent on the future of work than on the 'now' of work, and managers wonder why change is slow and good people leave.

This is a book about cultural evolution. It requires that you and your teams:

- define what you expect of each other in advance

- continually challenge the things that you do, and

- relentlessly ask the question, 'Can we do this differently?'

None of the world's great workplace cultures settle for 'business as usual' (BAU). BAU is where average results and mediocrity live. It's where innovation goes to die.

This book is about making your 'business as usual' continually better than it's been before.

BUSINESS AS USUAL

Before COVID-19, organisations came up with every excuse in the book to hold back change and maintain the status quo. Here are just a few examples:

- Pre-COVID, any investment in technology required extensive business casing and influencing up, down, left and right. Scepticism had to be endlessly overcome. IT managers cautioned against simply rolling out a tool as a mechanism for culture change, but were told to do it anyway.

- Pre-COVID, flexible working hours were seen as a luxury that only the large technology companies could 'afford'. People who needed more flexibility were required to justify their request, which then sat in someone's inbox for weeks waiting for approval. If it was granted, they were often still required to be online Monday to Friday from 9 a.m. to 5 p.m. – the very antithesis of flexibility.

- Pre-COVID, busyness reigned. There was little in the way of empathy for people's priorities, challenges or anxieties. Productive time shrank while expectations around outputs rose, and working 60 hours a week became a badge of honour, not a source of concern.

- Pre-COVID, innovation was considered a luxury. 'Hubs' were set up to satisfy those who demanded that innovation be taken seriously, when in reality, it lives inside everyone. People weren't given the time to challenge what wasn't working and the same mistakes were made over again.

- Pre-COVID, poor performance and behaviours were routinely ignored or excused. The safety of others wasn't a priority, or managers lacked the skills to deal with this issue in a calm, measured and empathetic way.

- Pre-COVID, senior managers were good at talking about culture being the most important thing, but made no money or time available to develop it.

COVID-19 challenged this approach* and gave managers the opportunity to redefine it in order to recover from the pandemic crisis quickly.

BETTER

Post-COVID, every organisation will face periods of uncertainty, but they also have the opportunity to fix the things that were broken in their 'BAU' culture. This is an opportunity to make a fresh start, culture-wise – and early action will determine whether lessons have been learned or whether the same old mistakes will continue to be made.

One of the things that's within an organisation's control is to agree on how people should behave, work together and make time for new ideas. They get to choose how they collectively face these challenges, and whether they emerge from the pandemic period as a more resilient, productive business that does more than just repeat, 'People are our most important asset'.

The humanity that we saw during the early days of isolation is now (rightly) expected within the workplace, as is flexibility, the use of technology and an openness to quickly changing some of the inefficient ways of working and the behaviours of people behind them.

Of course, money will be often be tight in a crisis situation, but making no investment in the things that are expected to carry you through it will be seen as a betrayal of trust and will undermine any emotional capital your organisation may have built up. Inefficient projects and other low-value activities should be cancelled or deferred to free up funds to ensure that the culture can be defined and then evolve in a positive way.

It's critically important that the learnings from COVID and future crisis situations are folded into a newly defined culture – one that values purpose over profit, safety over harmony and productivity over busyness. Research consistently shows that when employees are given the opportunity to define their culture, the organisation gets the results it's looking for. Any other approach will result in organisations continuing to suffer, and not just from the impacts of a pandemic.

HOW TO USE THIS BOOK

At the start of every chapter of this book, three actions to 'hack' your culture appear under the heading 'TL;DR', which stands for 'too long; didn't read'. In other words, if you read the chapter's title and think 'That's not for me right now', then you can simply read the TL;DR suggestions and move on to something more relevant to you. Not all of the hacks are going to be applicable to you, (particularly if you still have to socially distance from others), so focus on those that can provide immediate value.

I've then made a suggestion in each chapter of one thing you should stop doing. This is related to the hack and either frees up time to do the hack or else it's a ridiculous waste of your time that you should stop anyway.

Each chapter then contains background on the hack: a mix of origin stories, personal experiences, anecdotes, case studies, research and quotes. I explain the benefits of each hack, although it's up to you to decide whether you have the determination to go and get these benefits.

I've tried to think about all kinds of businesses in all kinds of places, so that there really is something for everyone.

This book was inspired by a YouTube series that I recorded, which can be viewed at youtube.com/colindellis. The videos are only a minute long, but they're useful if you want to read the book with my subtle Scouse accent in your head – or for sharing with members of your organisation to persuade them to bring me in to help. ☺

If you enjoy the book, I'd be grateful if you could write me a nice review somewhere, pass the book on or recommend to friends and colleagues that they should invest in their own copy.

If you'd like something regular from me in your inbox, you can sign up for my newsletter at:

colindellis.com/boom

If you do the social media thing, you can stalk, follow or connect with me at various places:

LinkedIn – linkedin.com/in/colindellis

Facebook – facebook.com/colindellis

Twitter – twitter.com/colindellis

Instagram – instagram.com/colindellis

And if you'd like to subscribe to my podcast for regular ideas from business leaders around the world on how they hack their culture, then search for *Culture Makers* on your favourite podcast provider and click 'subscribe'. Or you can find the provider links at anchor.fm/culturemakers.

Right, let's do this.

CULTURE HACK #1:
REDUCE YOUR EMAIL

TL;DR

- Turn off the notifications.
- Uninstall the email application from your phone.
- Set up a rule that sends all emails to the trash while you're on holiday.

ONE THING TO STOP

- Emailing people outside office hours.

Is there a business tool other than email that is both essential and so incredibly annoying at the same time? Email is like that family member who makes the very best cakes, but then gets trashed way too early in the party and everyone just wants them to go home (but leave the cakes, obviously).

When used properly, email is an effective method for communicating decisions or confirming conversations. However, it's incredibly annoying in that it's very rarely used properly, leading to hundreds of pointless messages being sent to you every day when a few 30-second conversations would have done the trick better. It becomes a drain on your productive time, and for some people, it's the bane of their lives – they have hundreds of unread emails in their inboxes and countless people are waiting for responses that will never come.

If you're looking to blame someone for your email problem, then Ray Tomlinson could be your man. An electrical engineer by trade, Tomlinson was working at the Department of Defense in the U.S. in 1971 on their Advanced Research Projects Agency Network (ARPANET), and he developed a method of sending an electronic message to someone else on the same network.[1]

Back in the mid-1960s, engineers at MIT had been using a tool called MAILBOX which allowed users to leave messages on a computer for one another, but Tomlinson's message was the first to be sent to another computer. By the mid-1970s, almost 75 per cent of ARPANET's data traffic was electronic mail – or email, as it became known.[2]

If you're interested in the technical details of how messages are passed from one computer to another across global networks, Wikipedia is the place to go. With the rise of portals such as America Online (AOL), the popularity of email rose dramatically. It even got its own movie starring Tom Hanks and Meg Ryan,[3] which took a quarter of a billion dollars at the box office – WTF?

As soon as email became mainstream, however, the spammers moved in and Nigerian princes quadrupled overnight. Scarily, some of these scams *still* rake in over $700,000 every year, according to CNBC.[4] It's estimated that US$1250 of productive time is lost per employee every year to opening and deleting spam emails.[5]

FREE UP YOUR FREE TIME

Frighteningly, the number of emails sent worldwide continues to increase. In my book *Culture Fix: How to create a great place to work*, I quoted 2019 statistics on email:

> *The definitive survey on email statistics is produced every year by The Radicati Group. In their latest report, they found that, 'The total number of business and consumer emails sent and received per day will exceed 293 billion in 2019, and is forecast to grow to over 347 billion by year-end 2023'.*[6]

Most organisations are doing nothing to reduce email or to set expectations around email use when people join them. There are acceptable use policies, but these tend to focus on what you can and can't say in emails, rather than how and when email should be used. Without this guidance, employees will conform to what others in the organisation do, and the number of emails sent or received or the time spent writing them often becomes a badge of pride. 'I have a thousand emails in my inbox!' 'I was up until 11 p.m. on Saturday replying to emails!'

This kind of culture can have a serious impact on employees' mental health. The Academy of Management found in a paper in 2018[7] that, 'Individuals who said they felt an obligation to check professional emails outside of traditional work hours also tended to report higher levels of anxiety and lower measures of well-being'.[8]

Some organisations are trying to do their bit. Car manufacturer Daimler has a routine set up that deletes employees' emails while they're on vacation. This is something that I copied myself to great effect.

I set up the following out-of-office message:

> *Thanks so much for your email, however I'm currently on leave until xxxx. If you require assistance, please contact xxxx, who is covering for me whilst I'm away. Please note that your email will be deleted. This is not because I don't view its contents as important, but rather because I can do nothing with it, nor do I wish to return from holiday to a thousand emails, thus affecting my productive time for my first month back.*
>
> *Thanks for understanding. (Also, you should copy this approach!)*
>
> *Colin*

I then created a rule within Microsoft Outlook to automatically send emails to the trash between the dates that I was away. The result: first day back, no emails!

Volkswagen is another organisation that has taken steps to block emails being sent outside of working hours, but more can be done by others.[9] France is leading the way by making it illegal for organisations of a certain size to send emails to its employees out of hours. Its 'right to disconnect' law[10] came into force in 2017 to halt the flow of information into inboxes over the weekend. Organisations can face fines and even prison time if they place unreasonable demands on their people. The legislation has been successfully implemented and is now a model being considered by other countries.

That's not to say, of course, that email is 'bad' when it comes to communication. It's just not the best form of communication for many messages. It's best used to confirm conversations or decisions or to provide information. It's no good for discussions, expectation-setting or performance management. However, these last three are the things that people want to avoid doing face-to-face, so they use email.

Some messages that you receive keep you up all night thinking about either their content or, worse, how to respond. Some are so badly conceived and written that you can't fathom what's actually being asked. Ashlee Vance's biography *Elon Musk* found the same was true of the Tesla founder: 'He's been known to obsess over typos in emails to the point that he could not see past the errors and read the actual content of the messages.'

We've all been there.

But seriously, if you're *actually* looking for someone to blame for your email problem, then you need to find the nearest mirror and take a good long look in it.

One government director that I used to report to said to me once, 'Colin, why is it that you don't have any emails in your inbox and yet I have hundreds?' I said to him, 'I rarely send them, whereas you can't go five minutes without dashing off your latest thought to a million people, who then "Reply All"… forever.'

Not automatically sending an email is a habit that has taken me years to perfect.

HOW MUCH IS TOO MUCH?

Email became a business tool for me in 1997. Prior to that, the jobs I had required me to use the telephone to communicate. When I was given my first email account, I wasn't told how it should be used, and I fell into the trap of using it to avoid conversations or to email my latest stream of consciousness.

I didn't give any thought to the person receiving the email, the structure of it or even why I was sending it in the first place.

My process was thus: have thought – write it down – think of the people who might be interested – copy them all in – click 'send'.

Some of these emails were important, but given the quantity being sent by myself and my colleagues, it became hard to determine which these were. There were no immediately obvious flags showing which emails I'd been copied into and which had been sent specifically to me, so all were opened (or not).

This only got worse over time, particularly with the introduction of the BlackBerry and then the smartphone. For the first time in my life, I was 'always on'. I'd had a laptop and a modem before, but nothing that I could put in my pocket that would continually alert me to its presence.

My last seven years as a permanent employee were spent working as a senior executive in government, where email is king. There is a strict 'cover your back' policy, so everyone really does get copied into everything – and don't get me started on meetings (that's later in the book!). I found it difficult to keep up.

Others found likewise. There were times when the office was likes a cross between an aviary and a clock shop, with whistles, bings and dings going off everywhere, and as soon as people got a notification, the phone would come out of the pocket.

Adam Alter, in his book *Irresistible: The Rise of Addictive Technology and the Business of Keeping Us Hooked*, wrote that 70 per cent of people check their email every six seconds. If you don't think you're one of those, ask yourself, why do you have notifications enabled on your phone?

Email notifications serve one purpose only: to distract you. In fact, all notifications serve that purpose, but especially email. Once you hear the 'ping' (or whichever ridiculous noise you have enabled) or see the little box rise from the deep (or drop in from the top) on your laptop screen, you can't help but be drawn to it. And once your eyes and thoughts have been drawn away from what you were working on, it can take as long as sixteen minutes to refocus – and that's if you don't get distracted again in the meantime.[11]

This constant onslaught of emails is not only demoralising, it has been proven to have an impact of minus 10 points on your IQ![12] Having tons of email in your inbox makes you dumb: fact!

In the face of the steady flow of email, I decided to turn off the notifications, and if I'm honest, it took a few weeks to get used to. I'd developed an unnecessary attachment to my own popularity and so kept pulling my phone out in the hope of a notification, before realising they were off. I then fell into another bad habit: relentlessly opening my email client.

So – having checked the company policy first – I uninstalled the email client from my phone. All of a sudden I wasn't 'on' all the time. Not only that, but I wasn't receiving or sending emails out of working hours and thus expecting it of others.

Senior managers often forget that they have a responsibility to set the example to others when it comes to communication. They should be role models of how to deliver a message, and that includes the times and ways in which the communications are delivered. While managers don't own the culture that they're part of, they have the ability to destroy it through their actions. Expecting staff to be 'always on' is one way in which they can have a negative impact.

Another problem with having so much email to contend with is that some messages are ignored or responses aren't provided. This is disrespectful to the people who sent them (the same is also true of not returning phone calls), but it's a symptom of having too many messages to deal with.

You can change your approach to email: you just have to want to do it. The decision to delete the email program from my phone changed my working life, as I regained control of my productive time. Pick a hack, stick to it, and make email your servant, not your master.

CULTURE HACK #2:
MAKE TIME FOR TEAMWORK

TL;DR
- Take the time to agree on how you'll work together.
- Decide on the behaviours you'll uphold.
- Commit to spending time on innovation.

ONE THING TO STOP
- Wasting time and money on teamwork activities that don't increase empathy or communication.

There's much to like about the Netflix culture deck. If you don't know what a culture deck is, it's essentially a document that outlines in clear and simple terms the culture 'rules' that the organisation's team agrees to adhere to – how they'll behave, work together and make time for new ideas – all in line with the organisation's vision and values.

Culture decks are informative, visual and contain enough detail to attract the kind of talent that you're looking for, while promoting your brand – and what the organisation stands for – at the same time. I use them in my own work and we've produced them for government, private sector and not-for-profit clients all around the world. They are unique and speak to the challenges or opportunities that each organisation has.

Anyway, where was I? Oh yes – there's much to like about the Netflix culture deck, not least this part:

> *On a dream team, there are no 'brilliant jerks.' The cost to teamwork is just too high. Our view is that brilliant people are also capable of decent human interactions, and we insist upon that.*[1]

See what I mean? The first sentence is such a great line, and makes the point that if you want to be a jerk who behaves poorly, doesn't meet deadlines or isn't a willing and able member of your team, then Netflix – or any other high-performing organisation that takes its culture seriously – isn't the place for you.

As Homo sapiens, we are hardwired to work together. All of the great achievements throughout history were the result of the combined efforts of many people; and yet, building a team isn't a natural act. It requires skill, courage, discipline and practice. All too often, however, the assumption is that not only do people know how to build teams, that they also know how to motivate and inspire each individual on the team and maintain the team's vibrancy.

This is not the case. Some people have a natural aptitude for building teams in the same way that some people have a natural aptitude for applied mathematics. But just like applied mathematics, how to build teams is a mystery to many.

Researchers Druskat and Wolff found in 2001[2] that there are three conditions that are essential for building teams:

1. trust between members

2. a sense of group identity and pride in the group, and

3. the belief that they are more effective together than apart.

To that end, building teams has to be a deliberate process that we teach people, so that they create the conditions for these three things to be present.

Most organisations, however, will set individual goals (or key performance indicators) that encourage and reward individual achievement rather than collaboration on group goals. Where a team has to achieve a goal, rather than an individual, there is an immediate acknowledgement that if there isn't an agreement on *how* they'll work together, they'll never achieve it.

Every successful sports team in history had a shared goal and also co-designed the culture required for the team to be successful. But it doesn't end there: it's only when the team members hold each other accountable to what's been agreed that they achieve that. This last point is often the difference between a championship-winning team and one with a losing record.

TUCKMAN'S MODEL

In 1965, American psychological researcher Bruce Tuckman was studying group dynamics as part of a small group of psychologists who were studying the behaviour of teams in the U.S. Navy. The group studied a plethora of different articles and research and, in conjunction with the observed behaviours, looked for patterns that they could associate with team-building.

Tuckman's resulting short article, 'Developmental sequence in small groups', was published in the 63rd edition of the *Psychological Bulletin* (pages 384–399) and has had a big impact on approaches to team-building around the world.[3] In the article, he outlined the four-stage process of forming, storming, norming and performing. He added a fifth stage, 'adjourning', to the model in 1977, but no-one really remembers that bit. He might even regret it, like having a tattoo of a nondescript flower or a quote no-one has heard of... 'The model was great until I added that fifth bit. I should have left it alone.' Or he might love it and wonder why no-one else does, who knows?

In my early working experience, Tuckman's model was applied as a theory rather than an evolutionary activity. That is to say, there was a series of activities we had to follow, which not only felt unnatural but also served as the latest management quick-fix to a problem that required nothing more than the management of a poorly behaving employee.

That's not to say the model is wrong: it's not. It's an incredibly useful starting point for team-building and often the easiest to grasp. Here's a 'brass tacks' view of Tuckman's four stages:

1. **Forming** – in this stage, people generally don't know where to start. They come into a team thinking about what they want from it, rather than how they can serve it. It's all about the 'me' and not the 'we'. The leaders within this forming phase start to demonstrate the behaviours that they expect of others within the team and take the lead on initiating activity that takes the group into the storming phase. For most people building teams, overcoming scepticism, cynicism and, well, dumb behaviour is the biggest challenge.

2. **Storming** – when people start working together in this phase, a couple of things start to happen. Firstly, people start recognising the skills that others within the group have (or don't have!). They start to understand their roles and responsibilities and look for guidance on the expected outputs. Secondly, friction starts to occur – and depending on the personalities and behaviours within the team, it

may occur a lot! Unhealthy friction leads to people not feeling safe, and a lack of safety leads to unproductive work. The aim is to avoid moving from storming to fighting or ignoring, which is easier said than done.

3. **Norming** – in the norming phase, people have said their bit, it's all been ironed out nicely, thank you very much, and they can get on with the job at hand. There's a focus on methods, processes and rules, empathy starts to occur naturally (in good teams, at least) and there's a sense of togetherness and belonging. Many teams get stuck in this phase and look to try to create continual harmony, rather than allowing thoughtful disagreement. In his book *Principles*, Ray Dalio described thoughtful disagreement thus: '…its goal is not to convince the other party that he or she is wrong and you are right, but to find out what is true and what to do about it'. Obviously, in environments where the manager is always right, thoughtful disagreement generally happens in coffee shops or bars and not at work, where it matters most.

4. **Performing** – to make it to this phase, team members have to be all in. One hundred per cent in. Not 80 per cent or even 95 per cent – they have to be willing to not only do their bit, but also to muck in and help others do their bit, too. Everyone should have everyone else figured out by this point, and the skills required to achieve the objectives should be known and in place. Challenge happens regularly and the group actively manages poor behaviour or performance, without the need for regular management input. Performing teams recognise that they're not the finished article and that if they don't show up with the right attitude, they'll let the team down.

TEAMWORK REQUIRES DELIBERATE ACTION

In 2019, Leah Ryder, then marketing manager of technology company Trello, wrote in a company blog post that a core pillar of productivity is 'A structured approach to the "how" of teamwork that solves basic team needs so everyone can feel free to clear away confusion and get the job done'.[4]

Without this structured approach, teamwork is left to chance. There's a 'cross your fingers and hope it works' mentality rather than a 'let's pause and take our time to do this right' approach. To achieve high performance, you need the latter approach. This deliberate action starts with understanding what the organisation itself is trying to achieve. What's its strategy, vision, values and goals and how does the work that the team is being asked to do fit into these? It's still possible to create a vibrant subculture of the overall organisation culture without this knowledge, but there's a danger that the team will become a silo that marches to the beat of its own drum.

Once it has this information to guide it, then the team must agree on the following six pillars in order to create the foundation for continued success. I cover each of these pillars in more detail in my book *Culture Fix: How to create a place to work.*

1. **Personality and communication** – everyone needs to meet everyone in the team (regardless of geographic location) and become familiar with their different communication styles. Empathy within the team is very hard to achieve without this meeting of minds and understanding of personalities.

2. **Vision** – at the heart of every great team is its aspiration. What does it want to achieve and how does this line up with what the organisation is looking to do? Teams with vision have purpose and intent, which fuels productivity and engagement.

3. **Values** – a set of statements about values provides emotional direction. Values are the glue that holds individuals within an organisation and provides direction for hiring, firing and decision-making. They aren't brand statements or commitments to do things you should already be doing. They're the beliefs that all within the culture hold to be true.

4. **Behaviour** – the human factors of interaction need to be agreed upon so that there can be no confusion on what's appropriate and what's not. An argument here is that people should already know how to behave, or that it's already been determined at a higher level so there's no need to repeat it. These are wrong, however: teams need different behaviours to achieve different goals. Plus, these behaviours give a team its identity.

5. **Collaboration** – the principles by which the team works together – the systems, processes, tools and mechanisms for meeting and sharing or challenging ideas – need to be agreed in advance. Leaving these to chance or hoping for organic growth will lead to confusion and loss of productive time. There's also an opportunity here to embrace different ways of working or to reject the current organisation culture norms in order to provide a point of uniqueness – for example, using the chat function on a collaboration tool rather than copying a thousand people into emails.

6. **Innovation** – without new ideas, new thinking or inviting different viewpoints on established ideas, the culture of the team will very quickly stagnate and the focus will shift back to 'me' not 'we'. Making time to be creative provides for problem-solving, opportunity identification, energy and excitement. And before you get all, 'Oh really, excitement?', you should know that I've seen it, frequently. And it's

awesome, because people genuinely care about making products and the way people work together better.

Happiness and a sense of belonging is the essence of what being deliberate about building teams is all about. So many team-building activities are, well, a bit shit. They're old-fashioned and often as sedentary as the people who deliver them. They do nothing to remove communication barriers between individuals, develop a collective growth mindset about what's possible, provide an opportunity for self-reflection and laughter, or give rise to a determination to get the job done in a way that will be talked about for years to come.

When you've learned how to build a team that does well, it's a skill you never lose. It's something to be shared, nurtured and kept up-to-date, because as history shows, when we work together, we can achieve anything.

CULTURE HACK #3:
PLAN IN PROCRASTINATION

TL;DR

- Set aside time to procrastinate as a team activity.
- Do something fun together at a random time of the day.
- Give your mind a break before focusing on the task at hand.

ONE THING TO STOP

- Being busy. It's boring and doesn't actually mean you're productive.

Oh, the irony of writing 2000 words on procrastination, minutes after spending two hours playing a computer game with my brother 17,000 km away.

Procrastination, according to Joseph Ferrari (Professor, General Psychology, Community Psychology at DePaul University in Illinois) is 'the purposive and frequent delay in beginning or completing a task to the point of experiencing subjective discomfort, such as anxiety or regret'.[1] I've used the word 'procrastination' a lot over my lifetime, and yet I'd never read a description of what it actually means before. (Obviously, this is true of most words, many of which I might be using incorrectly.)

The key words in the description are 'to the point of experiencing'. Every single person on the planet who's had any job, ever, has procrastinated. You might be doing it now, reading this book when you should be writing a report, practising a musical instrument or listening to your partner talk about their day. It's a necessary activity, but only to a point. Once you experience the 'subjective discomfort', then you have a choice to make.

You're experiencing subjective discomfort if, for example, you have thoughts that go like this:

- 'I should stop reading this now.'
- 'If I don't stop reading this now, then...'
- 'When I've finished this chapter, I really should...'
- 'I'll get to the end of this page, then I'll...'
- 'The report is more important, I should stop reading.'

Procrastination is a choice, and when done well, it can provide you with much-needed breaks in your otherwise hectic day. But when it's done badly, that's where anxiety, regret and (if we're being honest here) poor performance live.

According to the Project Management Institute (the global body for project managers),[2] 13 per cent of projects failed in 2018 as a result of team-member procrastination! I put an exclamation mark there; however, it shouldn't really come as any surprise.

The aforementioned Dr Ferrari is the global expert on procrastination and the curator of the Procrastination Conference. Research presented at the conference in 2017 found that 20 per cent of people are chronic procrastinators (or 'procs', as they're known in the trade).[3] A chronic procrastinator is someone who will go to extreme lengths in their business or personal life to sabotage their goals. That 20 per cent is apparently true of every culture, in every country in the world! (I had planned to check the facts as presented, but I got distracted.)

Back in 2016, Wenwen Zhang, Xiangpeng Wang and Tingyong Feng studied procrastination and published their findings in *Nature*.[4] They found that:

> *(1) the behavioral procrastination was positively correlated with the regional activity of the ventromedial prefrontal cortex (vmPFC) and the parahippocampal cortex (PHC), while negatively correlated with that of the anterior prefrontal cortex (aPFC). (2) The aPFC-seed connectivity with the anterior medial prefrontal cortex and the posterior cingulate cortex was positively associated with procrastination. (3) The connectivity between vmPFC and several other regions, such as the dorsomedial prefrontal cortex, the bilateral inferior prefrontal cortex showed a negative association with procrastination.*

Okay.

In layperson's terms, what they found was that procrastination is a product of our emotions, not willpower, and that two parts of the brain are involved in the processing of this information:[5]

1. The amygdala is a small nut-sized set of neurons that controls our emotional responses and is best known for controlling our fear response.

2. The prefrontal cortex makes up 10 per cent of the brain and is thought to control things such as planning, decision-making, problem-solving and self-control.[6]

The amygdala is always on guard. It's on the lookout for potential threats, and when it senses them, it releases hormones to allow you to 'flee' from them – including from things that you don't want to do. The prefrontal cortex, at the same time, is attempting to stop you from running away, because it recognises the sense of achievement you'll feel once you get those things done.

That's why procrastination often feels so difficult to overcome: the brain is literally fighting with itself while you scroll through your Instagram feed. If you fall into a cycle of chronic procrastination, the amygdala grows in size and reduces the effectiveness of the prefrontal cortex response.

Most of us have experienced chronic procrastination at some stage in our lives, and it can arise as a result of factors like:

- emotional stress
- lack of clarity
- boredom
- overwork
- distraction
- tiredness, and
- busyness.

It's the latter three that I see most in the individuals I work with. Our lives are full of things that can distract us these days, and most people allow them to do just that. There's a lack of discipline around the use of technology and people not getting enough rest, which is often a result of getting stuck in a cycle of being busy rather than productive.

There are many ways to overcome these issues, and discipline and courage are key to breaking the cycles. The courage to say 'no' when more work comes your way. The discipline to turn off phone notifications or to switch the TV off at a reasonable hour.

As I mentioned earlier, our lives are defined by the choices we make, and one of the biggest changes I made to my own life was to be deliberate about procrastination. I plan in time when I can walk away from everything, refresh myself, and then come back to whatever I was working on with renewed vigour. I credit planned procrastination for the reserves of energy I can muster up after three days of being on my feet speaking in front of large groups, and for the clarity I can find when reading or writing.

In an article in the *Brain and Cognition* journal in 2016, researchers were able to show that an eight-week program of meditation actually reduced the size of the amygdala,[7] which helps you to be more attentive and override the need to 'run away' from a task. Meditation is something that I have personally taken up, so I can attest to its effectiveness.

PUT YOUR BRAIN ON PAUSE

Not long after I moved to Australia with my family in 2013, I took a role heading up a project-delivery department for a government agency in Melbourne. As with my other roles, I wanted to start by building on all of the good things that the team did already, while taking steps to define the culture we needed in order to be successful for the next 12 months.

I had a new industry to learn, people to meet, government rules to become familiar with, people issues to deal with, technology to learn and (along with my wife) I also had to settle our young family into a new country and culture.

I resisted the cultural norms of endless meetings and emails in order to free up some thinking time and to make myself accessible to people – and yet, before long, I found myself eating lunch at my desk and working until everyone else had left the office, then heading home to flop on the sofa, grab a whisky and play some FIFA before bed. The next day, the cycle would start again.

It wasn't long before the procrastination started. I allowed my mind to wander during meetings, started skim-reading important reports, wasn't actively listening in stakeholder meetings and missed important deadlines. It was utterly unsustainable, and after a visit from my parents (itself exhausting!), I decided that I needed to establish a routine to give my mind a break.

I blocked out time in my calendar at 10.30 a.m., 12.30 p.m. and 3 p.m. to grab a drink, go for a walk and change my environment. I'd take a 15-minute walk while listening to music or an audiobook, and if it was raining, I'd simply walk between our two buildings and go up and down the stairs. At lunchtime, I'd jump in my car and drive down to the river nearby. I'd put my phone into airplane mode and then play a meditation track for 20 minutes. In the first week, I used to fall asleep in the car, but as I started to go to bed earlier, this gradually changed and I was able to stay focused on my breathing and clearing my mind of the clutter.

Around this time, I read a book called *Emotional Capitalists* by Martyn Newman. In it he said, 'When your mind is calm and clear, you will be more creative and alert'. Within two weeks I was as productive as I've ever been.

BE AS WELL AS DO

My timed walks and meditation were the best kind of procrastination, as they meant I gave my eyes a break, too. There's still an old-fashioned view about meditation in some work cultures, when in reality it's a practice that can add great value to a culture.

Google famously employed a Jolly Good Fellow (an actual job title!) whose role was to 'enlighten minds, open hearts, create world peace'. Chade-Meng Tan was an engineer and helped to develop Google's first mobile search engine, but his real passion lay in helping people to achieve success and happiness. His *New York Times* bestselling book *Search Inside Yourself* has been endorsed by the Dalai Lama, ex-Presidents of the U.S. and CEOs of some of the greatest workplace cultures in the world.

If you're still unconvinced, or you're sceptical of the way that large technology organisations do business, then consider the most annoying droid (don't get me started) in the *Star Wars* universe: C-3PO.

In the novelisation of *Star Wars: A New Hope*, when Luke, C-3PO and R2-D2 go to visit old Ben Kenobi, Threepio says, 'If you'll not be needing me, I think I'll shut down for a bit. It will help the armature nerves to knit, and I'm due for some internal self-cleansing anyhow'.[8] So there. If it's in *Star Wars* it must be a good thing to do, right?

(I wonder if this is the first time that Chade-Meng Tan has been mentioned alongside C-3PO? I must ask him.)

The mindfulness practice established within Google has been replicated by cultures all over the world to help staff take a break within the working day, in order to increase their happiness and, by happy coincidence, productive time.

However, most workplace cultures are perennially stuck in a cycle of 'do, do, do', and very few ask themselves if this is actually producing meaningful outputs that contribute to the organisation's overview vision in a way that's sustainable.

Doing can only ever be sustainable if time is made for being as well. In his book *The Art of Living*, author Thich Nhat Hanh wrote: 'We have a tendency to think in terms of doing and not being. We think that when we're not doing anything, we're wasting our time. But that's not true'. He went on to say, 'So as well as saying, "Don't just sit there – do something!", we should also say, "Don't just do something – sit there!"'

Group meditation sessions are a great idea, but you don't have to do them to procrastinate together as a team. You can go out for breakfast, grab a coffee, go for a walk, play a board game, take up a hobby, check your social-media feed, phone a friend, listen to music or watch a TED Talk. Just do anything that takes your mind away from what you're doing, and don't apologise for it. By undertaking these activities as a group, you get to know each other better, create accountability, develop shared stories and ensure that you're able to get the best out of each other. You also set the benchmark for others to follow.

Once the time for procrastination is up – and you'll know when it is, because you'll feel the subjective discomfort – then it's time to get back to work, refreshed and ready for what the rest of the day has to throw at you. Then, you just have to remember to put yourself to bed at a reasonable time… provided you don't get distracted along the way.

CULTURE HACK #4:
TRANSFORM YOUR MEETINGS

TL;DR

- Inject some creativity into your meeting structure names.
- See who can have the least number of meetings in a week.
- Block out time for productive work.

ONE THING TO STOP

- Booking meetings for 30 or 60 minutes – that's Outlook laziness. Think about the time you actually need and book your meeting for that time period instead (even if it's six minutes!).

I hear all the time that 'meetings are an important structure for decision-making and progress evaluation', and I never disagree, as it's a true statement. It's just that when you have seven meetings a day (most either 30 or 60 minutes long) and they run back-to-back and are either dominated by people who lack respect or else don't offer you the chance to talk, then I call bullshit.

One survey found that as many as 30 hours per month[1] are wasted on unproductive meetings; when you multiply that by the potential productive output of the attendees of those meetings, you have a big problem. But like most inefficient legacy structures, most organisations just keep on with it in the hope that the next meeting will sort itself out. (It never does.)

Some organisations are good at creating rules for their meetings that they print off and leave in meeting rooms; however, the principles are rarely followed and eventually become coasters for coffee cups. As General Stanley McChrystal said in his book *Team of Teams*, 'The rules for any meeting are established more by precedent and demonstrated behavior than by written guidance'. This is true of the good and the bad ones.

Over my 30 years of employment, I went to my fair share of meetings and I generally had two issues with the rubbish ones:

1. They weren't well defined.
2. They weren't well managed.

Most organisations suffer from both of these issues at the same time, which is why meetings have the reputation that they do. They become a source of frustration and stress, and people lose sight of what they exist to achieve.

Auditors are now attuned to looking for unproductive meetings to highlight how poor leadership or inefficient practices led to the demise of something. The construction of a children's hospital in Perth, Western Australia is a case in point. This was a project that was originally planned to be completed at the end of June 2015. The date was moved to the end of August 2015 and then again and again and again, until the hospital finally opened its doors in May 2018, almost three years late.

There was mudslinging, as there often is with poorly managed projects, but the effects on the public were huge, as they were paying $8.2 million per month for a hospital that wasn't taking any patients. The report on the project by the Public Accounts Committee[2] detailed the endless governance meetings that occurred between ministers, the Department of Health, the Department of Treasury, the taskforce appointed to lead the work and their subcontractors. They found that ministers accepted advice and information without question and that '…reporting repeatedly failed to convey the gravity of the situation on the ground and was often excessively optimistic'.

Summarising their findings into the failed project, the Public Accounts Committee made the following statement:

> *Confusion around key roles and responsibilities continued to plague the governance structure well into 2017. We find it difficult to comprehend how this confusion was not resolved throughout the almost four-year, 156-meeting, life of the Perth Children's Hospital Commissioning and Transition Taskforce.*

One hundred and fifty-six meetings. And there was still confusion.

Unfortunately, for the clients that I'm approached by, this type of practice is normal and accepted. It doesn't have to be this way, though.

Now, if all of your meetings are productive, personable and punctual, then great job, proceed immediately to Go, collect your $200 and move on to the next chapter – your work is done. However, if just one of your meetings sucks, then read on – if only to be reminded of the things you should do in order for this face-time to be successful.

MEETING DEFINITION

If we accept that putting people together in a room (or virtually) to have a discussion that results in either a decision or information being shared is critical to the smooth running of a business, then defining why you need a meeting in the first place and who should attend is crucial to its success. As Dermot Crowley said in his book *Smart Teams*, 'If a meeting is worth holding, it's worth planning'.

By putting deliberate thought into why a meeting is required, you're respecting not only your own time, but that of others. You're asking yourself the following questions:

- Why is this meeting required?
- Why now?
- What are the goals of this meeting?
- What is the minimum number of people required to achieve these goals?
- Who are the people?
- What other priorities might they have at the minute?
- What preparation is required in order to achieve the goals?

Of course, it's much easier to find a free hour in the calendars of 20 people and send out a meeting invite, 'blocking' the time out for a discussion about something to be advised or TBC. Much easier and much lazier.

This was a practice that I didn't allow in the teams that I managed. Every member of staff had permission to decline any meeting invitation that didn't provide the purpose of the meeting, the preparation required and an agenda. It didn't matter what seniority a person had; if they couldn't demonstrate that they'd given thought to people's time and the intent of the meeting, then you could simply reject it.

This completely changed people's approach to meetings. Almost overnight, there were fewer of them. People recognised that most meetings weren't required at all, as you could simply walk up to someone's desk or pick up the phone and either have a quick chat or arrange to have one later. Indeed, these informal meetings often strengthened relationships and generated richer discussions. The formality of the meeting structure had been rejected in favour of having an evolving conversation in a much safer space.

Four walls, a set of chairs and a door that shuts aren't always required. It's what gets discussed and agreed that matters.

Where the formality of a meeting is required, then it may require more than sending out an invite with all the details in it. You may have to have conversations with certain people to ensure they understand the meeting's intent and to gain their commitment to attend. Simply sending out an invite won't get this.

MEETING MANAGEMENT

I worked in government for eight years and I have to say that people were pretty good at meeting definition. Given the auditing requirements placed upon us, there were always itemised agendas, minutes from the last meeting and reading materials to prepare people for the decisions that would be involved. It's just that people were absolutely appalling (and I'm being generous here) at managing them.

The chair of the meeting was often late, and even when they were on time, they would then wait for everyone else to arrive rather than starting when they should. Side conversations were allowed, phones and laptops were being used (and not for taking notes), people were just rude and spoke over the top of each other, while other people were never brought into the discussion.

The meetings then ran over time and everyone stayed, rather than respecting their next engagements. They never finished with a summary of the decisions made and the actions to be followed up on by a named individual – and before you knew it a 'follow-up' meeting had been scheduled with all of the same people to discuss the very things that should've been discussed in the first meeting! I'm getting cross just writing this.

During the COVID-19 crisis, this kind of poor meeting management simply moved online. Most organisations realised that the ill-discipline was present regardless of the format, and that the issue is one of behaviour – as the mechanics of what makes good meeting management are well known, and have been for years.

Virtual meetings, just like in-person meetings, need to be managed so that everyone gets a say, issues are discussed in a way that generates decisions, and everyone leaves with a full understanding of what needs to be done next and who has responsibility for it. Every meeting should feel safe, too. There should be no dominant person generating fear or making people feel uncomfortable.

Elon Musk has garnered a reputation as someone who does just that. Indeed, in her biography *Elon Musk*, author Ashlee Vance records a member of staff at Tesla describing Musk's behaviour in meetings thus:

> *We'd have these meetings and take bets on who was going to get bloody and bruised. If you told him that you made a particular choice because 'it was the standard way things had always been done,' he'd kick you out of a meeting fast. He'd say, 'I never want to hear that phrase again…'*

I'm all for not doing things in a standard way, but 'bloody and bruised' we can do without in work.

I think lazy meeting management undermines productive time and there is simply no excuse for it. On the plus side, with the application of a few hacks to the way you currently do things, you can change everything overnight:

- You can start and finish your meetings at random times.

- You can have a late jar (with donations going to charity) for those that don't make it on time.

- You can start each meeting by sharing a staff story in line with your values.

- You can build in appreciation moments where you share thanks for work done.

- You can take your meeting outside, rather than inside.

- You can record your meetings to hold everyone accountable.

- You can set a shorter time limit and stick to it.

One of the things that I like most about the Scrum methodology for delivering products is the focus on short, sharp meetings. Those of you who've been doing short, sharp meetings for a while will rightly claim that this is nothing new; however, managers love a good method and Scrum is the latest method of choice.

In a Scrum meeting (yes, named after rugby scrums), every person answers three questions:

1. What did you work on yesterday?

2. What are your priorities for today?

3. What's in your way?

One person speaks at a time, there are no side conversations and only those with tasks are allowed to talk. The whole thing should last no more than 15 minutes. If you want to introduce a bit of energy and fun to these meetings, you could throw a ball to each other or else, as the U.S. company Menlo Innovations does, pass a Viking helmet to the next person to speak. The last person to speak at a Menlo stand-up meeting finishes proceedings by saying, 'Be careful out there'. And they're done.

Other meeting mechanisms that you can use include:

- **PechaKucha** – which means 'small talk' in Japanese. This is an event where people present slideshows of 20 pictures in 6 minutes and 40 seconds, with each image being shown for exactly 20 seconds. People have to think about exactly what they want to say and then stick to it. It's great for showcasing new ideas.

- **World Café** – this is a creative structure to help with the sharing of knowledge around a particular subject. The group is split into smaller groups, then after a short period of time everyone moves to different tables, with only one person remaining on each as a host. This structure ensures that the exchange and challenge of ideas is fast and captured for future discussion.

Finally, there's really no need to give your meetings boring names. This demonstrates a lack of creativity and makes them sound unappealing and, well, boring. I haven't met a person yet who wants to attend an 'Audit Meeting'. Alternative names include, 'Under the Covers Meeting', 'Is and Ts Meeting' or, if you want to add a touch of humour, 'Trap Door Gathering'. It's easy to be cynical about this kind of thing, but why be boring when you can be interesting?

Most meetings aren't rubbish, but the way that they're defined, managed and named often is. Don't fall into this trap.

CULTURE HACK #5:
GO ON A FIELD TRIP

TL;DR

- Network with or visit organisations whose cultures you admire.
- Share with others what works in your culture.
- Stay on top of what's new and test it in your culture.

ONE THING TO STOP

- Trying to copy other organisations' cultures. Take an idea and apply it to your context instead.

Inigo Jones was born in Smithfield, London, in 1573. His father (also named Inigo) was a cloth maker, but other than that little is known about his early life.[1] Indeed, you may not have even heard of him; however, if you've ever visited London and specifically Covent Garden, you will have stood in the middle of some of his most influential work – but I'll get to that and its relevance to this chapter.

The young Inigo became a joiner and then an artist, and in his early 20s, decided to visit Italy to draw inspiration from the great artists there at the time of the Renaissance. The Renaissance became the bridge from what is referred to as the Middle Ages to the modern age, and was a period of almost continual change.

Some of the greatest artists, thinkers, authors and scientists came to prominence at this time and Florence, in particular, was considered to be the birthplace of the Renaissance. The wealthy Medici family bankrolled many creatives and people journeyed from far and wide to see the works of Leonardo da Vinci, Michelangelo, Bernini, Titian and (my personal favourite) Caravaggio.

People visited cities such as Pompeii, Rome, Naples, Venice, Paris and Geneva studying the artwork, sculptures and architecture that each had to offer. It became known as the Grand Tour. Items were purchased and shipped all over the world, but the greatest triumph of a Grand Tour was the inspiration it provided to the traveller to do great things when they returned home.

Grand tours inspired Mary Shelley to write *Frankenstein*, Mark Twain to write *The Innocents Abroad* and Johann Wolfgang von Goethe to write *Italian Journey*. Their influence can also be seen in movies such as *A Room With a View* and, of course, *National Lampoon's European Vacation*! More recently, actors Steve Coogan and Rob Brydon have used the Grand Tour concept as the inspiration for their hit TV series *The Trip to Italy*.

The Grand Tour inspired Inigo Jones, too, and he became the first professional architect in England, in the modern sense of the term.[2] He did two tours – in 1596–97 and 1605 – before he reached his mid-30s. On his second tour, he particularly studied the drawings and architecture of Palladio, and he introduced the Palladian style upon his return to England. The most spectacular example of this – and of Jones' work – is the Banqueting House, built in 1622 and still standing magnificently in Whitehall in London. Its gilded, hand-carved timber ceiling frames a masterpiece by Rubens (added in 1635–36 and the only surviving example of an in-situ Rubens ceiling anywhere in the world) and was inspired by the ceilings that Jones had seen on his grand tour.[3]

The redesign of Covent Garden square (including St Paul's Church) was one of his next projects and is often considered to be 'more Italian' than some of the great Italian palazzos![4] St Paul's itself was modelled on a Tuscan temple in the style of Vitruvius. The influence of Jones' travels can be seen in the arcaded houses that surround the square, with their beautiful facades.

In 1615, Jones became James I's personal surveyor – quite the responsibility in the 17th century – which meant that he had an architectural say in everything that the crown commissioned, such was his standing. He died in 1652, aged 78, but his influence lives on and has inspired generations of architects and artists to see the world in search of inspiration.

GET OUT TO GET INSPIRED

So does this mean that you and your team should head to Italy? Of course it does! But only if you take me with you. I'm a good laugh and can hold my wine. Promise.

But really, I'm encouraging you to broaden your horizons. Get out into the world and find out how other people do things; it's really not that hard. In all the books I've written so far, I provide many case studies of organisations that do culture well. Most of these are excellent at sharing and some even run tours so that you can see exactly what they're doing to engage and inspire their people and how they do it.

In 2019 I attended the Zappos Culture Camp in Las Vegas along with about 35 other people. Throughout the three days, they showcased their culture. They had senior leaders (although they don't call them that) tell us about the things they do. They talked about how they uphold their values, how they celebrate success and how they make sure the same mistakes aren't repeated. They invited us to their all-hands meeting and gave us the opportunity to ask their CEO, Tony Hsieh, questions about how he's been able to maintain the Zappos culture now that they're part of the Amazon family.

It wasn't 'cheap' (especially given the travel and accommodation costs), but then learning, growing and developing never is.

Of late (and given the rise of the Agile movement), senior managers have been jumping on planes and heading to Sweden to visit the offices of Spotify. Spotify's engineering culture is unique, and yet when I first read about it in 2013, it cost me absolutely nothing.

When I was a senior manager, I was constantly on the lookout for different things that people did to lift engagement and productivity, regardless of the organisation that I was working for or the city I was in. That's not to say that I was permanently restless or thought we were inefficient; it's just that as an early adopter, I wanted to try things that I felt would help us to work smarter, not harder.

As I was working in government, I didn't have access to thousands of dollars to spend on travelling, extensively searching for great cultures. Indeed, all of our learning and development funds were used on team – not individual – activities. So I did the only thing that I could do: I networked, read, watched and listened for ideas that could help us to work together better.

I read an article by Spotify engineer Henrik Kniberg in 2013 called 'Spotify – the unproject culture'[5] (take a look: it's still available and still relevant at the time that I'm writing this), which lays out quite clearly the culture of delivery that Spotify has. I shared it with the team and we decided which ideas we'd like to try out.

Obviously, we weren't Spotify, and it's important to keep that in mind whenever you read about what others are doing. You can't simply copy someone else's culture and structures; many organisations have found this out the hard way. For example, Netflix published their culture deck in 2009 and, given the growth of their business in the early 2010s, senior managers rushed to copy what they'd done. However, without people with a growth mindset, a set of shared values and the context within which the culture is defined, it's almost impossible to copy what anyone else does, including if you want to simply introduce new team names.

FIND YOUR COMMUNITY

The thing that I found invaluable in my search for new ideas was networking. Now, networking – that is, mixing and mingling in a room with like-minded people, often with canapés and wine – is not for everyone. I'm naturally extroverted, so found it easy to walk up to someone and say, 'Have you ever implemented SharePoint? Oh, you have? I'd love to buy you a coffee and find out about your experiences of doing so.' (This is a true story. Back in 2008, the company I was working for wanted to do just this, so I made it my goal to find another organisation that had done it so we could find out what went well and also learn from their mistakes. The information we were able to gain from them contributed significantly to our success.)

However, in-person events aren't the only way that you can do this now, and thanks to the generosity of practitioners and organisations around the world, there's a great deal of information being shared in the public domain. Organisations such as Atlassian, Culture Amp and IDEO (to name just three) are fantastic at sharing what works well for them and providing simple things for others to try. They never say, 'We're right, we've got it nailed!', they say, 'This has worked for us in this area, doing this piece of work; it could work for you too'.

There are also groups you can join on LinkedIn and Facebook that can provide you with insights; however, in my experience they're full of 'noise' that serves only to distract.

In late 2019, we launched the Culture Fix Community (culturefixcommunity.com). We wanted to create a safe space for practitioners to share information, ideas, research and case studies on what's worked for them with other people in the same position around the world.

We recognised that it was increasingly difficult for people to find what they were looking for and to build connections with others virtually who could act as valuable sounding boards for their ideas. Having a community of people around you who share your passion and purpose provides you with a sense of belonging and safety. You understand that you're not in this alone, and that not only have others been on a similar journey, but they can share with you what they do in the hope that it's useful.

In order to evolve culture in a positive way, then, you have to continually look for new ideas everywhere. A field trip is a great way to see how others behave, collaborate, innovate or set their working space up for success, but if money or time is scarce, you can do it just as effectively from your laptop.

CULTURE HACK #6:
BE HONEST, ALWAYS

TL;DR

- Schedule an honesty half-hour.
- Create a safe space for people to talk honestly.
- Make feedback constructive, not critical.

ONE THING TO STOP

- Lying or being liberal with the truth. Seriously, stop it.

We have hard conversations. We know we'll never achieve our mission if we aren't communicating openly and honestly with each other. Honest feedback delivered frequently and with good intent is what helps us build better products and developer better leaders.

— Sheryl Sandberg, Facebook

Do I have to write a chapter about the importance of being honest? Really?

Okay, I know you're probably reading this for a friend, but I can't stress enough that honesty, when done well, can spur people on to great things, help us to see the humanity within others or else help us to heal wounds and move on from an issue.

In a survey conducted on honesty by AYTM in 2015, 90 per cent of the respondents agreed that honesty was a positive trait for people (quite what the other 10 per cent thought is beyond me), and yet only 54 per cent agreed that most people were generally honest. Only 40 per cent agreed that businesses were honest, so it's clear that there's some work to do, across the board, on honesty.[1]

In 2010, the Science Museum in London[2] conducted a survey on lying with 3000 British men, and let me just say, before I share the results with you, that they do not represent the author, regardless of how British he is. It found that on average, men tell at least three lies every day, compared to women, who lie twice. Over the course of a year, it's estimated that men lie 1092 times per year compared to women who lie 728 times. Like I said, the results aren't representative of the author.

Of course, the caveat to this latter survey was that people think that it's okay to lie to protect or defend someone, or if they've been given a gift that they don't like! And there's the rub with honesty: we all seem to have a different opinion of what it means.

The phrase 'honesty is the best policy' is often misattributed to William Shakespeare, when it fact the first written proof of it is in the publication *Europae Speculum* in 1599 by Sir Edwin Sandys, an English politician and colonial entrepreneur.[3] He wrote, 'Order may reach a note higher than our grosse conceipts, who thinke honestie the best policie, and truth the only durable armour of proufe'.

In 2020 language, he's basically saying, 'If in doubt, you know, when the chips are down and all, you better tell the truth, because, well, it's the right thing to do. Obvs.' And of course, telling the truth and being honest is the right thing to do, it's just that sometimes we become liberal with it in order to avoid confrontation, upset or hurt, or to protect someone we care for. Which, of course, is the wrong thing to do. My mum always used to say to me, 'Beware your lies will find you out', and like most children, if I did something wrong or made a mistake there was never a consequence for that, but if I lied about it then I was in a world of pain (sometimes literally).

While being honest can often feel like the hardest route to take, in the long run it is always the correct one. If we're able to be honest with ourselves, honest with others and have honesty in what we do, then it gives rise to a number of benefits:

- According to a 'Science of Honesty' study, it can improve mental and physical health.[4]

- According to a Harvard study, it can help you improve your standing as a leader.[5]

- According to *Psychology Today*, it improves your relationships with others.[6]

All that simply by not lying. So why do we do it? Often, it's peer pressure – the need to say or do something to stay 'onside' with everyone else. To not rock the boat or be seen as different. If this is your fear, then let me tell you the story of Honest Eddie.

HONEST EDDIE

John Edward Murphy (nicknamed 'Eddie') was an exceptional baseball player, and was a member of the championship-winning Philadelphia Athletics in 1912 when they defeated the New York Giants. He stayed in Philadelphia until 1915, when he was traded to the Chicago White Sox – though if he'd known what awaited him four years later in 1919, he might have tried to stay put.

Now, back in 1919, the clubs owned the players and despite bringing in huge crowds, the players were poorly compensated for their efforts. So, some of them decided to take matters into their own hands.

The 1919 Chicago White Sox was an exceptional team and made it all the way to the World Series. If you're unfamiliar with baseball, this is their cup final. Oh, and for clarification, the 'world' being referred to in the title is actually just North America. Anyway, they were really good, but felt that they were being deprived of the financial rewards that such a season should offer them by the club's owner, Charles Comiskey.

A number of the players decided to try to rectify that. First baseman Chick Gandil acted as go-between with a gambling syndicate led by loan shark Arnold Rothstein, who promised the players $100,000 between them if they threw the upcoming World Series against the Cincinnati Reds. As the dressing room was already divided, only half of the team were aware of the fix and of them, only eight agreed to participate. Eddie Murphy was not one of them.

When the fix was exposed after the Reds surprisingly took the series 5–3, the White Sox players were investigated. At this point, it would have been easy for Eddie to tell the story that he'd been told to tell, but he refused. He resisted the peer pressure and instead chose to distance himself from his teammates and co-operate fully with the investigation. He was exonerated, while eight other players received life bans and were henceforth known as 'the Chicago Black Sox'.

Eddie Murphy's honesty was lauded and Charles Comiskey sent him a letter stating, 'The honest ball player is stronger today than ever', along with a bonus of $1500 – a huge amount of money in 1919.[7]

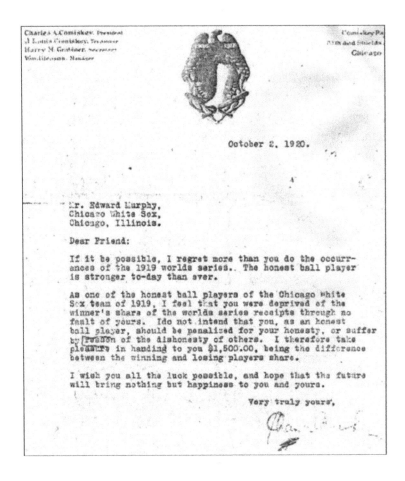

He was given the nickname 'Honest Eddie'. His home town of Hancock, in upstate New York, honours his memory with a statue in Town Square Park and a bar named after him, where you can get 'an honest drink, at an honest price'.

MAKING HONESTY EASY

So if honesty is the best policy and we reward people for their honest behaviour, how do we make it a habit within our organisations? Well, like most skills, it starts with training, continues with practice and ends in accountability.

In his *Harvard Business Review* article 'Don't be nice; be helpful', *Four Seconds* author Peter Bregman wrote that the way to create a culture in which people are 'open and honest for each other's benefit' is to share feedback often.[8] Not twice a year as part of an annual review process or when someone's done something wrong, but continually, so that not only do people become comfortable providing feedback, they become comfortable receiving it.

Any human interaction should start with trust. It should never have to be earned; it should be assumed. When we expect the worst of people, that's often what we get. However, this trust can only be maintained if expectations are set in the right way and we understand the communication preferences of the other person, so that we're able to provide feedback in a way that they will appreciate, not push back against.

In my book *Culture Fix*, I went into great detail about how communication is a skill we presume everyone has, but that in reality, it's picked up from our parents and our friends, who often don't provide the best examples of how to do it well! When feedback is provided in a way that another person doesn't appreciate, it can be seen as insensitive, too direct or confusing. Worse still is when it's overtly critical. The phrase 'constructive criticism' is an oxymoron, often used by morons. There's nothing constructive about criticism, as it's still criticism of another human. However, when feedback is delivered in the right way, an honest assessment of performance or behaviour can absolutely be constructive if you're also able to help, coach and support the other person in achieving what needs to be done.

Honesty requires safety, which means that it has to be a central part of the way that you do things on a daily basis and there is no fear of consequences for expressing a contrary opinion or idea. To create safety around honesty in the teams that I used to manage, we instigated honesty half-hours. In these sessions, we'd offer up factual assessments of the things we'd observed about each other, both positive and negative. When you were on the receiving end of the feedback, your job was to listen, make notes if you needed to, then say thank you.

Of course, the first couple of times you run through this exercise it feels strange and ever so slightly confronting. By the third time, though, it starts to feel utterly natural, and before long the honesty half-hours can be dropped altogether, as honesty becomes part of the daily routine and it feels safe to provide immediate feedback.

You know when humans are bad at things, because a specific day is created to remind you to do important stuff that you should be doing every day. Regardless of whether it's love (Valentine's Day), mental health (R U OK? Day) or showing respect to our elders (Grandparents Day), these things should be part of our everyday lives and not something we do once a year.

Similarly with Honesty Day, which occurs every year on 30 April – so picked because the first day of April celebrates falsehoods.[9] It was the brainchild of M. Hirsh Goldberg, author of *The Book of Lies: Schemes, scams, fakes and frauds that have changed the course of history and affect our daily lives.* Which is probably about eight words longer than it needs to be, if I'm being honest.

In reality, every day should be Honesty Day. You gain the respect of everyone you come into contact with if you can be empathetic, honest, willing to listen and open to opportunity. This is when you're at your best and where great teamwork flourishes. It's not cruel to provide honest feedback; it's cruel when you don't.

CULTURE HACK #7:
MANAGE STAKEHOLDERS UNIQUELY

TL;DR

- Collate fast facts about people you need to build relationships with.
- 'Map' your stakeholders to better understand how they feel.
- Present the information in a creative way.

ONE THING TO STOP

- Wasting time producing a stakeholder-management plan that contains no information about their personality or how they like to be communicated with.

There's a mistaken view that stakeholders are a unique set of people who are easily identifiable and can be managed as a group, rather than individually. Often within business, stakeholder management is actually defined by how information is disseminated, rather than how it is consumed.

The reality is that if someone chooses to be a stakeholder, then they are. Every member of staff is a stakeholder, and every member of the public also has the opportunity to be a stakeholder. And if you haven't done any work to identify who they are and how to build a connection with and communicate to them, then there's a good chance that you'll have a negative interaction with them.

Consider the COVID-19 case study of Britannia Hotels in the U.K., which managed to ignore both of these things and suffered the consequences.[1] On Thursday 19 March 2020, as the reality of the COVID-19 virus became evident and people around the world started to isolate, the Coylumbridge Hotel in Aviemore, Scotland (part of the Britannia Hotels group) sent more than a dozen letters to staff informing them that their employment had been terminated and that they had to vacate the hotel (essentially their home) immediately.

The announcement meant that immigrant employees had no income, nowhere to stay and due to the restrictions, couldn't get home. A copy of the letter was published on Twitter[2] by Andrew Thomson of BBC Scotland and it also stated, 'Please understand that if you have taken more holidays than you had currently built up an allowance for, then this amount will be deducted from your final salary, as per the terms and conditions of your contract of employment'. Thomson recorded Highland Council convener Bill Lobban as describing the action as an 'absolute disgrace' and saying that the hotel was 'throwing staff on to the street with no hope whatsoever of returning to their home countries'.

The fact that Britannia Hotels didn't treat its staff with empathy and kindness, as you would any stakeholder in the business, at a time when they needed it most, is unforgivable.

Of course, to these kinds of organisations, employees are simply a commodity. They don't recognise that if they are to succeed, then they not only need the engagement of employees, but they also need to continually build emotional capital with them, such that they're able to perform at their highest level.

In their report 'Making work more meaningful: Building a fulfilling employee experience',[3] professional services company PwC stated:

> *[Employees] have individual needs which an organization must meet if it's to succeed in the competition for talent and drive innovation. A more personal relationship with employees has paved the way for a work experience that goes beyond traditional measures of commitment, satisfaction, and discretionary effort...*

They're basically saying that you can't treat your employees like shit, and if you do, there'll be a consequence. And of course, for Britannia Hotels, the consequence was almost immediate following the sharing of the aforementioned letter – because in a world where it's easy to share your experiences, the general public is also a stakeholder. The backlash against the hotel group was swift and fierce. The story was picked up by all of the major news outlets. Interviews were undertaken with affected staff, while hotel management went to ground and battened down the hatches in the hope that it would go away. It didn't.

Mentions of Britannia Hotels ran into the hundreds of thousands, reviews were left on the hotel website calling their treatment of staff 'shameful' and Scottish Tourism Alliance CEO Marc Crothall waded in as well, saying:

> *There is huge anger among our industry as well, this is not reflective of how all of our businesses that we know and our members behave. Hundreds and hundreds have come out to condemn what is a deplorable action.*

Other hotels stepped in to offer to house sacked employees as the area rallied around those affected. And still no word from Britannia. That came the following day, when the chance to contain the story had long since passed.

A hotel spokesperson said (as reported by the *Liverpool Echo*),[4] 'Unfortunately, the communication sent to these employees was an administrative error. All affected employees are being immediately contacted. We apologise for any upset caused'. And that was it.

Of course, by then it was too late. Thousands of people had decided that the way the group treated its staff meant that they could no longer stay at a Britannia hotel in the future. BBC presenter Andrew Neil, who has over a million followers on Twitter, said, 'I suspect many folks, when they see this, will be adding Britannia Hotels to the list of businesses they will not be frequenting when this crisis is over'.[5] The tweet garnered 38,000 likes and almost 14,000 retweets, bringing it to the attention of thousands of potential stakeholders.

STAKEHOLDERS ARE YOUR AMBASSADORS

Mary Shapiro, in her book *HBR Guide to Leading Teams*, said, 'If your stakeholders like what they see, they'll spread the word'. This is why you should consider all members of staff to be stakeholders, as well as those who have a direct impact on the work that you're doing or are directly impacted by it.

Organisations need to be deliberate about how they interact with their stakeholders, so that they can not only build emotional capital but also ensure communication is clear, specific to their needs and provides confidence that their expectations will be met.

And that all starts with employees.

According to American analytics and advisory company Gallup, 'Organizations have more success with engagement and improve business performance when they treat employees as stakeholders of their own future and the company's future.'[6] Great working cultures do this really well. They find ways to build connection between their people to make communication easier.

Back in 2019, I interviewed Didier Elzinga, CEO of Culture Amp, in the company's Melbourne headquarters for my *Culture Makers* podcast. In the office's reception area were huge TV screens, and while Didier and I posed for a photograph, images of staff scrolled through the screens once a minute, profiling who they were: their location, skills, interests and preferred pronouns. It was hypnotic. I could have stood there for an hour getting to know their people.

The information gave employees a 'face' and provided information beyond a role title. It created a sense of belonging, togetherness and humanity – which are all essential for a vibrant workplace culture.

American billionaire hedge fund manager and philanthropist Ray Dalio, in his book *Principles*, describes how his organisation Bridgewater Associates went about a similar exercise. They created 'baseball cards' that provided information on each member of staff.

This is something I do in my work with organisations today, encouraging them to capture information about staff such as place/country of birth, birthday, preferred pronoun, achievements, things they're good at and outside interests. You could also add other things such as sports teams, favourite magic trick, favourite music concert… anything really that helps staff to build connection and gain a better understanding of each other.

The most important element to capture, however, is how your stakeholders like to be communicated with – something that organisations are inherently lazy about in most of their work.

EMPATHY MAPPING

There is a misplaced assumption that everyone consumes information in the same way. Most communication breakdowns occur because people didn't think about how the different stakeholders needed to hear the message in order to understand and accept it.

If we accept the fact that all humans are different (even identical twins), then we must also accept that simply sending an email to multiple people and hoping they all get the same message is doomed to fail, forever.

Carl Jung, in his work on personality in the 1920s and 1930s, found that we are essentially a mash-up of four different types. There are people who like facts, data and proof. People who like to understand the value of something and who want to be treated with warmth and empathy. People who want logic, an element of risk-taking and for messages to be delivered directly without excess words. And people who care for creativity, energy, context and camaraderie.

When written in those terms, it's easy to see that the 'one size fits all' approach to communicating with stakeholders won't work. The easiest way to understand stakeholders' communication requirements is to ask them, 'How do you like to be communicated with?' It's better still if they tell you up-front.

This is something I used to do when starting a new job. I told my team not to email me or copy me into emails if a conversation would suffice instead, and that face-to-face or phone conversations were the best way of engaging me. For my part, I made the time for people to do this throughout the day and got to learn their preferences, too, so that I could modify my style (not the message).

We also employed a technique called 'empathy mapping', which is a way of better understanding your stakeholders to ensure that your communication approach is fair and balances the interests and needs of all.

It's a method best described by Emrah Yayici in his 2016 book *Design Thinking Methodology*. The book is written for software engineers, yet it's applicable to all areas of business. In it, he explains:

> *As UX [user experience] professionals, it is our job to advocate on behalf of the user. However, in order to do it, not only must we deeply understand our users, but we must also help our colleagues understand them and prioritize their needs. Empathy maps, widely used throughout agile and design communities, are a powerful, fundamental tool for accomplishing both.*

The empathy maps that I encourage clients to use today are split into four separate quadrants that capture the different elements of stakeholder engagement – Says, Thinks, Does and Feels:

1. **Says** – these are the things that your stakeholders express out loud: quotes, sayings, acronyms and stories.

2. **Thinks** – these are the thought processes that your stakeholders have throughout the engagement. Of course, it's possible to have duplication between Says and Thinks; however, there may be some thoughts that people aren't prepared to share. These are often the most important things to capture.

3. **Does** – these are the actions that stakeholders take. What do they do and how do they do it? What do their processes (deliberate or otherwise) look like?

4. **Feels** – often the piece that is missing with traditional stakeholder mapping is understanding how a person may feel at any given time – what excites them, worries them, energises them or keeps them up at night.

Remember that this information could be different for each individual within a particular stakeholder group. This is why great stakeholder management takes time, effort, energy and continual evolution.

Britannia Hotels could have very quickly managed the situation in March 2020, had the management team better understood and cared for their stakeholders. Accepting the challenging business conditions at that time, they could have had one-on-one conversations with affected staff, looked to rehouse them elsewhere, provided immediate emotional and financial support and attempted to secure alternative employment for them.

They could then have sent a clear message to their public stakeholders about their actions and how they were treating humans with empathy and understanding, further reassuring people that they were doing all they could to grow their business through humanity and humility. That they didn't do this is likely to have serious ramifications for their business, because stakeholders never forget a bad experience and go to great lengths to tell others about it.

CULTURE HACK #8:
INDUCT AND ONBOARD TO IMPRESS

TL;DR

- Be available to new hires.
- Organise an induction rotation around the organisation.
- Involve your whole team in the induction process.

ONE THING TO STOP

- Making people sit in front of a PC to read the intranet.

According to HR consulting organisation Wynhurst Group, 22 per cent of staff turnover occurs in the first 45 days of employment.[1] They also found that new employees who go through a structured onboarding process are 58 per cent more likely to stay with the organisation for more than three years. I'd say those are pretty compelling statistics. What the survey doesn't say is that the 58 per cent who choose to stay are the people you need to keep in order to positively evolve the culture to where it needs to be.

However, most organisations aren't all that flash when it comes to onboarding. Only 12 per cent said their organisation did a good job at it, in one Gallup survey,[2] and when I think back to my own experiences in this area, that feels about right.

In all of the jobs that I ever had, I can only think of three really positive introductions to my new organisation. Most were average or just downright disengaging, to the point where after only one week I was thinking, 'What have I done?' I'd been through a structured interview process in which several senior people put on their best show. They talked about challenge, possibility, opportunity, talent, culture, engagement and evolution. And yet there I was on day one, without any introductions, equipment, information or even a boss to provide these things.

So, you do what you can to get through your first day. Walking, listening, talking but mainly wondering why anyone in their right mind would spend so much time 'selling' a role to you and then pay no attention to those initial couple of weeks, which provide the foundation for success – or at least help you to integrate into this new culture.

As the old advertising slogan goes, 'You never get a second chance to make a first impression' – which I suppose is true in both a positive and negative sense. Building a sense of belonging starts on minute one of day one, and if the opportunity is lost it may never return, leading to early attrition and a sense of 'what could've been'. It's easy to dismiss the people who leave early as 'not a good fit' or something similar, but the question must always be asked: 'What could we have done differently?'

Most onboarding experiences start with the expectations that are set during what we now call 'pre-boarding'. This includes the messages the organisation puts out about its values and its culture (see Culture Hack #24), the way it treats its people and the information it provides to its stakeholders.

How is the job advertisement written? If outside agents are used to recruit, how is the organisation ensuring that its values are being upheld and people aren't simply being thrown into a large machine that hopes to spit out a couple of suitable candidates at the end of the process?

Once candidates have been selected, what does the interview process look like? Is it staid, old-fashioned and boring? Does it use standard questions, even if you're hiring for uniqueness? Does it reflect the kind of role you're hiring for or the person that you're looking for? Have you done a good job of helping candidates to prepare so that time isn't wasted?

How people are brought into an organisation is a crucially important part of the employee experience. In fact, often this is the very thing that shapes the experience.

The LEGO Group is a Danish toy-manufacturing company that does a fantastic job at pre-boarding and onboarding, and also very generously shares everything it does to provide inspiration to others who are looking to provide a similar great experience to potential employees.

LEGO© builds fun into its pre-boarding, so that people get an early understanding about what the company is about and what they can expect. The aim of any pre-boarding experience is to filter out those people whose values don't match yours, as it's really hard to do this once someone is on the payroll. Sometimes it's possible to do this in one or two interviews; however, some of the great cultures around the world often don't put a limit on the number. It can be four or five – whatever it takes to ensure that they get the right values fit. It's not a 'bums on seats' numbers game for them, it's all about values match.

Back to the LEGO Group. During the recruitment process, people may be asked to build something (using LEGO©, obviously), which serves to emphasise the importance of play within the culture. If you don't want to 'play', then it's good to find that out before you're given a desk and taken on a tour of the office.[3]

MAKE IT PERSONAL

Zapier is a global remote-working company based in Sunnyvale, California. While its headquarters is located there, its 250-plus staff are located in more than 24 countries. It is a true remote-working organisation, so onboarding is something that has to be handled differently.

It is clear about its purpose:

> We want to empower businesses to create processes and systems that let computers do what they are best at doing and let humans do what they are best at doing… We believe in small teams… Small teams mean less bureaucracy and less management and more getting things done.[4]

It is specific about the kinds of people that it's looking for in order to maintain the service levels it has. For Customer Champion roles, for example, only 2 per cent of applicants get a job fit interview and of those, only 0.4 per cent are hired. This means that 98 per cent of applicants never get to the interview stage.[5]

Once at the interview stage, it's really down to the candidate to have done their homework to be able to demonstrate how they'll add value to the organisation.

The Muse published a great guide to pre-interview preparation[6] and listed five key things that candidates should focus on:

1. **knowing the company's strong suits** – vision, values and anything else you can glean from the 'about' section of a webpage

2. **sniffing out its financial health** – investor relations, financial reports, stock market assessments, recent acquisitions, funding rounds and so on

3. **watching community interaction** – what is the company saying on social media? What kinds of knowledge does it share and where does it 'hang out' with the people it's looking to engage?

4. **going undercover to learn company culture** – seek out company profiles, culture videos or culture decks or check employee-review websites such as Glassdoor

5. **reading up on the field and competitors** – make sure you know what the organisation is up against, what challenges it faces and what opportunities it has.

Organisations such as Zapier specifically look, in the first interview, to see if candidates have done their homework and given some thought to how they would fit into the organisation. It wants to ensure there's a values match before conducting a second interview on skills.

For many organisations, by comparison, there's only one interview and it's purely skills-based. Often – due to their own poor planning – organisations need someone quickly, and anyone with a pulse and the technical skills to match the job they're looking to fill will do. Skipping the values-match stage always leads to trouble later down the line, however.

Zapier conducts three interviews and bases its decision on values match and skills. If interviewers don't feel that they've got the right person for the role, then they'll start the whole process all over again. Throughout this process, there is constant communication and the organisation promises it will never leave it more than seven days without letting a person know where their application is at.[7]

If you make it through the interview process, then references are checked – again, not on the skills that the person has, but the kind of human being they are. Once people have satisfied those criteria, then they're in! Some may consider this to be a long-winded process, but anyone who's worked in a consistently vibrant culture will recognise the importance of this approach.

BE GENEROUS AND UNIQUE

How do you live up to that approach once people walk through the door? Well, by creating an induction process that is unique, tailored to the individual and worth talking about and sharing.

My LinkedIn feed is often full of people starting new jobs for great cultures, sharing pictures of the welcome they received from the team, the swag that was on their desk waiting for them and other experiences they were treated to.

A quick search of the term 'onboarding swag' will return hundreds of search results that outline the lengths that organisations go to in welcoming their new employees – T-shirts, mugs, key-fobs, M&Ms, personalised notebooks, pins. During the COVID-19 crisis, construction company Picquette & Howard Electric Service Inc., based in Plaistow, New Hampshire, included face masks, bandannas and hand sanitiser with their regular bag of swag![8]

Of course, all the swag in the world won't ever replace the human interactions people have on their first days, weeks and months in a new job. At LinkedIn, new hires write their name on a sticky note with a headline describing them as a professional, as well as an interesting fact about themselves (just like you would do on your LinkedIn profile). They have sessions called 'Investing [In] You' which cover important stuff employees need to know about the way the organisation works and the perks that they're entitled to. There's also a campus tour, lunch and a series of executive talks, so that new hires gain a full understanding of the organisation before they even start work. Oh, and there's swag, and equipment that works.

Twitter strategically places new hires' desks next to key teammates they'll be working with, who help, coach and support them as they settle into the organisation. There's a monthly happy hour for new hires with the senior leadership team and a rotating schedule of presentations to bring them up to speed.

Once, when I started a job, they had neither the equipment that I needed to do my new job, nor a desk for me to sit at. So they put me in a meeting room, with a folder of information to read! I still get flashbacks to those two days – oh yes, I spent two days doing that until my boss arrived on the Wednesday!

The very best onboarding programs provide inspiration, motivation and collaboration and generate a fire that's hard to put out. These experiences are shared around the world, which in turn creates a desire from great employees to work for these organisations in the future. A great onboarding program not only safeguards against losing great employees before they get started, it also provides an endless talent pool from which these cultures can continually draw.

And that's an experience that everyone benefits from.

CULTURE HACK #9:
FAIL VISIBLY

TL;DR

- Find creative ways to recognise when things go wrong.
- Share what you've learned from failure.
- 'Celebrate' that you won't make the same mistake again.

ONE THING TO STOP

- Failing fast. I know it feels like heresy to say this, but you don't know what opportunities you may miss if you draw a line under something too quickly.

My friend Levi doesn't like the suggestion that failure should be celebrated. I agree – unless you're deliberately setting out to fail, of course, in which case go for your life.

The Google team behind the moonshots program (simply called 'X') are constantly looking to break things and fail. According to CEO Astro Teller, there's even excitement around this![1] But in my experience, organisations such as X are very much the exception.

I like what Reid Hoffman, co-founder and former executive chairman of LinkedIn, said on this: 'We don't celebrate failure in Silicon Valley, we celebrate learning'.

So, we're clear: 'celebrating' failure is (mostly) bad. However, only good things – and by that I mean continual learning – can come from making failure visible. Yet, like most things in the business world, it's not something that's done well. Mostly, we try to avoid failing because of the way that it feels, and yet, paradoxically, if we don't ever fail, then we never grow or learn. So it's important that we make our peace, personally, with failure. Or, as Friedrich Nietzsche said in *Twilight of the Idols*, '*Was mich nicht umbringt macht mich stärker* (What does not kill me makes me stronger)'.

Except – and not wanting to rain on Nietzsche's parade here – it's not always true that failure makes us stronger. Sometimes it causes self-doubt, fear and anxiety and gets in the way of future progress, and of course, that's mostly the brain's fault.

In a *Psychology Today* article,[2] neurologist Judy Willis is quoted as saying:

> *As you internalize your thwarted efforts to achieve your goals and interpret them as personal failure, your self-doubt and stress activate and strengthen your brain's involuntary, reactive neural networks. As these circuits become the automatic go-to networks, the brain is less successful in problem-solving and emotional control.*

When we fail, sometimes the brain heads down a slippery slide, and as we found when we were children, it's often really difficult to climb back up it without slipping down again.

One way to overcome this, according to research,[3] is to fight the temptation to think that it's all going to end in failure and have a growth mindset instead. When it comes to mindset, of course, Carol Dweck is the expert that the world turns to. In a 2016 study[4] that she undertook with Kyla Haimovitz, she found that when children were encouraged by their parents to see failure as an opportunity for learning and growth, they were able to bounce back more quickly than if their parents enforced a mind-set of 'failure is bad'.

Another thing that we can do to avoid the slippery slide is to have a contingency plan in case of failure. Many organisations that I work with are great at capturing risk. Some people seem to like nothing more than running a lengthy risk workshop ('Hopes/Dreams Workshop'? See Culture Hack #4) and then filling in a big spreadsheet with lots of words that no-one will read. Oh, and that doesn't mention any kind of meaningful action that could be taken to mitigate the things that could go wrong.

Planning for perfection is also a recipe for disaster. Something, somewhere will go wrong and if you accept that, then research[5] says that you're better able to recover and not make the same mistake again. Projects are one area where perfection is expected. Most organisations measure how successful they've been by assessing whether they delivered on time and to budget from the original data in either a business case or original project plan. However, at the business case stage, not enough is known about the detail of what it will take to deliver the products or services (whatever they may be), and at the original planning stage we simply refine the data in the business case to a better degree of accuracy, not a perfect target.

As a former head of a project department myself, we used to say that at business case stage the costs and timescales are plus or minus 100 per cent of current estimates. At original planning stage, the goal was to get the degree of accuracy down to plus or minus 15 per cent, which in itself is a stretch given the unknowns at this early stage.

Even though, as a government agency, we had to report time and cost targets to the regulator, internally we measured the success of our projects on how happy the stakeholders were, which is something that Spotify does as well.

We recognised that while we might not come in on time or meet cost targets – and please don't mistake me here, we were extremely disciplined as a team in attempting to hit these targets – we could create a fantastic team culture that recognised that things may go awry and if they did, then we'd put plan B into action to address the failure.

Having said that, there are organisations that seem to be great at failing at the same things over again, which should always be a cause for concern and force people to look at their culture and how it needs to change. One very simple thing that these organisations could do is make their failures visible.

SHARING IS CARING

Late one night in 2011 at the offices of commercial data, analytics and insights organisation Dun & Bradstreet Credibility Corporation in Malibu, California, CEO Jeff Stibel got frustrated. He had a great team of people who were good at their jobs; they just lacked one crucial element to become a truly vibrant culture, and that was the ability to take risks. He felt that he'd created safety within the team (i.e. there was no blame or finger-pointing in any way), but he just couldn't empower people to take the leap of faith.[6]

American comedian and talk show host Ellen DeGeneres said about failure and risk-taking, 'It's failure that gives you the proper perspective on success. When you take risks, you learn that there will be times when you succeed and there will be times when you fail. Both are equally important'.

Jeff Stibel knew this, but try as he might, he couldn't instil this into people, so he decided to do something radical. He bought a tin of white paint and a brush and used it to cover an entire wall. On that blank canvas, that night, he and his wife stencilled quotes about failure from famous people in the hope of inspiring risk-taking. There were quotes from Robert F. Kennedy, Thomas Edison, Charlie Chaplin and Michael Jordan.

He left a pen by the wall and headed home. The Failure Wall had been created, and within days it had taken on a life of its own. Not only did staff add their own failures and quotes to the wall, but when stakeholders visited the offices, they would spend time in front of the wall reading about the things that others had done and asked if they could add theirs, too.

Pretty soon afterwards, calculated risk-taking started to occur more frequently and the HR team incorporated a question on failure into their review process. By 2012, the group had achieved double-digit growth and the wall was getting jam-packed with learnings.

Stibel cites the wall as the organisation's opportunity to fail forward[7] – that is, to make mistakes but to pass the learnings on to other people so that they don't do likewise. If you search for 'Dun & Bradstreet failure wall', you can see an image of the original wall.[8]

I'LL SHOW YOU MINE...

Creating an environment where failure is okay is a core part of vibrant workplace cultures. If there's no emotional (or physical) fear, then people will take calculated risks. Innovation thrives on calculated risks, so it's up to managers everywhere to ensure that it's 'safe' to take them.

A lack of safety is often why innovation hubs don't work. The intent is often good – 'Let's do something to generate the conditions where creativity can thrive' – however, if employees see blame being apportioned to anything, anywhere in the organisation, it will inhibit their actions. The organisation will always get what it always got and those ideas will never see the light of day.

Continual innovation is what gave the lubricant WD-40 its name. The solution we use today is the 40th iteration and ergo, the one that works best. I'm sure there'll be a WD-41 at some stage – and if anyone from WD-40 is reading this, if WD-41 could clean the toaster, that'd be awesome.

Being vulnerable and sharing your failures will encourage others to do the same. Indeed, in many interviews, asking about failures is becoming standard. It's something I used to ask when hiring in the early 2000s.

The shortest interview I've ever conducted happened in 2011. The first question I asked in interviews was, 'Tell me about any failure and what you learned from it'. I used it as a bit of a loosener for the candidate, a way to get them to open up, after which I would do likewise and talk about something I'd learned from my past, and we'd share a human moment. The agents acting on our behalf to prepare people for the interview had briefed everyone in advance, so it was usually a nice, easy way to start.

On this particular occasion, however, the candidate said that he'd never failed. I made sure that he understood the question before asking him again. He thought for about five seconds and repeated the same answer. My fellow panellists and I looked at each other and nodded sagely, then we thanked him for his time and ended the interview there and then.

It's something that's important for Google ANZ Managing Director Melanie Silva, too. In an *Australian Financial Review* interview in 2019, she was asked what the most important question was when hiring a new member of staff. She replied, 'Tell me about your biggest failure. Some people can't resist telling you about how they turned a failure around and end up sharing a success story, others describe the disaster and what they learnt from it. The best tell you how they've adapted or changed because of it'.[9]

Self-aware people will be open and honest about their failures and some will even find the humour in them. People with low self-awareness will often assume that failure is seen as a sign of weakness and should never be divulged, when in reality, it's our humanity that brings us closer together and the weakness lies in not sharing. Or, as *New York Times* bestselling author Brené Brown said, 'Our job becomes to get specific on whose opinions matter and find the people who love you, not despite your vulnerability, not despite your imperfection, but because of it'.[10]

CULTURE HACK #10:
CREATE A BOOK GROUP

TL;DR

- Create a leadership library at work.
- Introduce some structure into what you're reading.
- Create an event to share what you've learned with others.

ONE THING TO STOP

- Being a content vacuum. Be deliberate about what you read and look for learnings you can put into practice.

I was watching *Blackadder* on TV with the kids recently. If you're not familiar with it, then have a word with yourself: it's simply not good enough that you haven't seen this fantastic four-season historical comedy. It was written by Ben Elton, Richard Curtis and Rowan Atkinson, who also stars in the show as the lead character.

We were watching Episode 2 of *Blackadder the Third*, called 'Ink and Incapability', in which the Prince Regent (expertly played by Hugh Laurie) decides to become patron of the new book by Dr Samuel Johnson (played by future Hagrid, Robbie Coltrane), simply called *Dictionary*. Which, incidentally, Edmund Blackadder thinks is the most pointless book since '*How to Speak French* was translated into French'. I'm laughing just typing this.

Anyway, halfway through the episode, Dr Johnson retires to Mrs Miggins' Literary Salon to mix with his bookish chums and admirers Byron, Shelley and Coleridge, and they talk loudly about the merits of the aforementioned *Dictionary*.[1]

While the writers' main aim was to get people laughing, they are also incredibly clever people: Curtis and Atkinson graduated from Oxford and Elton from the University of Manchester. They wanted the shows to be as historically accurate as possible, and in 18th-century England (when *Blackadder the Third* is set), book clubs were extremely popular.

Now, one could argue that they were merely convenient structures that encouraged drinking, drug-taking, gossip and raucous behaviour[2] (as was portrayed in the show), but were they really that different from the book clubs of today? Well, yes, of course they were… well, for the most part at least. The key difference, of course, is the fact that books are much easier to get your hands on today than they were in 18th-century England.

Literary clubs were springing up in America in the 18th century too. In 1727, aged just 21, Benjamin Franklin organised a club in Philadelphia following his return from a trip to London. He modelled the club, which was called the Junto, on the coffee shops that he'd frequented in England. The group donated their own books – as buying them was expensive – and created their own library. Not satisfied with the number of books in the library, Franklin pooled the membership funds of the Junto and used them to buy books for everyone to read.

For the club's meetings, Franklin generated a list of questions which included the following:

* *Have you met with any thing in the author you last read, remarkable, or suitable to be communicated to the Junto?*

particularly in history, morality, poetry, physic, travels, mechanic arts, or other parts of knowledge.

- *What new story have you lately heard agreeable for telling in conversation?*

- *Hath any citizen in your knowledge failed in his business lately, and what have you heard of the cause?*

- *Have you lately heard of any citizen's thriving well, and by what means?*

Franklin was very proud of the Junto and wrote of it in his autobiography: 'Our club, the Junto, was found so useful and afforded such satisfaction to the members that several were desirous of introducing their friends, which could not well be done without exceeding what we had settled as a convenient number', which was twelve.

The club was a place of learning, where successes and failures could be shared, adding to the richness of the information and creating a network of like-minded people dedicated to their improvement and that of others as well.

As a footnote to this story, in 1732, Franklin hired what would become the first ever librarian to curate the books that the Junto had collected.[3]

OPRAH

In the mid-90s, reading became en vogue once more and book clubs came roaring back into our lives, thanks in large part to Oprah Winfrey. Author Jerry S. Herron was effusive in his praise:

More people are reading books than at any time in the history of American society, without contact with the so-called authorities. Oprah has done a brilliant job of encouraging people to do that.[4]

From 1996 to 2011 (with the exception of 2002), Oprah's Book Club was a monthly segment of the hugely popular *Oprah Winfrey Show*, recommending 70 books and creating much debate and no shortage of controversy along the way. One author, Jonathan Franzen, dared to dismiss the club, saying that his novel *The Corrections* was a 'hard book for that audience'. I know! He said that out loud! He apologised and then got stuck into a huge slice of humble pie when he appeared on the show the following year to discuss his latest book (which Winfrey had chosen!), *Freedom*.[5]

Millions of Americans created mini book clubs of their own to debate Oprah's choices, leading Scott Stossel of *The Atlantic* to write, 'There is something so relentlessly therapeutic, so consciously self-improving about the book club that it seems antithetical to discussions of serious literature'.[6] But the discussions continued, even after the show ended (although it returned as *Oprah's Book Club 2.0* for Apple TV in 2012).

The clubs, as they had in the 18th century, became places of discussion, debate and disagreement, providing an opportunity for people to build connection and create something that they were proud to belong to. They also became a place of learning.

Their membership was often a closely guarded secret and you had to know a friend of a friend just to get an invite. It was like the Masons, but diverse, up-to-date and relevant. American humourist Emma Bombeck joked about trying to leave a book club, saying, 'Getting out of the hospital is a lot like resigning from a book club. You're not out of it until the computer says you're out of it!'

Book clubs became so popular that they even got their own movie called (imaginatively) *Book Club*, with a story centred on the book *Fifty Shades of Grey*. The comedy starred Jane Fonda,

Diane Keaton, Mary Steenburgen, Candice Bergen, Craig T. Nelson, Andy Garcia and Don Johnson, and grossed over $104 million at the box office. At one stage it was third in the top 10, behind *Deadpool 2* and *Avengers: Infinity War*![7]

A COMMUNITY OF LEARNING

Book clubs aren't a place for speed-reading: they're a place for reflection, understanding and learning, and they're a wonderful community for organisations to encourage. By their nature, book clubs are informal and are best when their membership is diverse. If they become closed shops they tend to be seen as cliques, which doesn't translate well in workplace culture.

Of course, there doesn't have to be just one club in an organisation – there can be many – and they don't have to just discuss books. It can be articles people have read, TED Talks they've watched, webinars they've attended – anything at all, providing that the emphasis is on learning, discussion and action.

I've been a member, set up a couple and also (as an author) been asked to attend to explain my thinking or the inspiration behind my work (which is always fun to do). In my experience it's important to have a set of guiding principles for your book club that link to the values of your organisation. If the rules are too rigid, however, they'll put people off attending, so you want them to be inviting. Here are some key principles that you can copy:

1. **Stay true to the purpose** – I think it's a great idea for the group to agree on the purpose at the first meeting. The purpose is a statement of the good that the book club exists to do, so might be something like, 'We promote continual learning for all our members'. Something like that, but not that! For it to mean something to the members, they have to come up with it.

2. **Create a book list** – I was part of a club once which had a twelve-month list, and while that was good (as every person got to pick a book), we found that after three months a number of new books had been released that we wanted to read! So we moved to a three-month rolling list instead, with someone rostered on every month. You had to provide a month's notice of what the book was so it could be ordered, downloaded or hired. Of course, someone created a spreadsheet and very useful it was, too.

3. **Have a code of conduct** – I know this sounds a bit draconian, but it's essential if the purpose is to be achieved. These will include such items as: 'You must read the book' (always important!), 'You must prepare a three-minute summary of your thoughts and have one key learning', 'No-one can interrupt while someone is talking', 'Polite disagreement is encouraged', 'Small talk happens once the meeting has finished'. Something like that, although again, the group should determine these. The meeting chair should rotate based on who chose the book – to keep things simple – and the chair has to keep order.

4. **Make time for fun** – as well as a place for learning, clubs are also a place for laughter. Unless you're reading *Angela's Ashes* or *The Road,* of course (which you should do by the way), when the tissues won't be mopping up laughter tears. Have a glass of wine, go to each other's houses, do it over lunch: just make sure that it's not super serious. Remember, the power of book clubs lies in their informality and the safety that you co-create so that people are confident to share what they thought.

5. **Plan in advance** – you want to avoid the 'Whose turn is it this week?' scenario where you all love attending the meetings, but you don't actually organise them very well.

Once everything has been agreed and the rota set, it should go into people's diaries as soon as possible, so that everyone has advance knowledge of when they'll be chairing.

It doesn't really matter what books you choose, as you're building relationships and creating shared stories, which do wonders for culture. By focusing on business content, however, you can stay one step ahead of what's new or else dissect the opinions of the latest release or popular video. Better still, you could build up a 'library' of books in the office. Find some shelf space, have a simple mechanism for checking them in and out and then ask people to share what they've learned with others before replacing a book and selecting a new one.

Like I said, though, it doesn't matter really, as long as you take your time and think deeply about the words that you're reading. In our information-rich world today there's a tendency to skim-read most things in order to obtain a shallow knowledge of everything. However, you only get the benefits of reading if you take your time. Those benefits include:

- reduced stress
- lower blood pressure
- mental stimulation
- exposure to new ideas or emotions
- improved knowledge
- improved vocabulary, and
- better focus and concentration.

Dr Seuss wrote, 'The more that you read, the more things you will know. The more that you learn, the more places you'll go'. When you do it with a group of people, it can only enhance the experience.

CULTURE HACK #11:
HOLD A HOBBY EXPO

TL;DR

- Find something that ignites your creativity.
- Share your passion with others.
- Find ways to indulge your hobby with a group of like-minded people.

ONE THING TO STOP

- Not making time to hear how people spend their leisure time.

I used to be a trainspotter. There, I said it. My therapist said it would be good for me to get that out into the open to heal my wounds.

I'm not feeling it yet, mind. Maybe because I still have the pictures of me, my dad and brothers at an out-of-the-way restored railway line or on a cold platform at Crewe Station in the middle of England. Being in the centre of England, Crewe was the place that all trains went through and Dad wasn't shy about dragging us to the end of the platform to see which engines we could 'spot'.

Dad had been a trainspotter as a kid. When I asked him recently how that had happened, he said that his family weren't blessed with money (possibly the biggest understatement in this book) and not far from where he lived there was a train line where they could watch the steam engines roar past. It became something that he enjoyed doing. He and his brothers also stole coal from the station's coal yard as kids, but thankfully he didn't develop that hobby any further.

So, when he had three boys of his own, he decided to indoctrinate us in the ways of the locomotive, and honestly, I have some fond memories of that time. We went to railway yards, would sit in the car drinking tea waiting for a certain train to pass and whenever we were on holiday (always in England), we would find the nearest platform and see what we could see. It was Dad's way of getting away from the stresses and strains of life and provided an opportunity for adventure, often with similarly anoraked individuals with cameras and notebooks.

I haven't spotted any trains for about 35 years now.

While we were off trainspotting, playing or watching football (still my main hobby today), Mum was at home knitting. When we were young, everything we wore was either knitted or handed down from other children! Well, not everything, obviously. Mum had a bag with all her knitting gear in it, which lived under a table in the corner of our living room; whenever we went out, the bag came out. When we came back, she was often in exactly the same place that we'd left her and the jumper she was working on would have gained an arm.

I asked her once – very possibly in a moody teenager kind of way – why she liked it. She said that it was an escape from her thoughts and her day-to-day chores. She had to focus on the knitting 100 per cent and couldn't allow her mind to wander, otherwise she'd have to redo hours of work. One study that I read when researching this book actually found that 74 per cent of people who took up knitting found it to be both calming and therapeutic.[1]

Julia Roberts is one example of a famous person that knits, while others have different (and some odd!) hobbies:

- Tom Hanks collects vintage typewriters (are there any other kind now?).

- Leslie Mann rides a unicycle.

- Jim Carrey paints.

- Susan Sarandon plays table tennis.

- Will Smith fences.

- Taylor Swift makes snow globes.

- Brad Pitt makes pottery.[2]

EVERYONE SHOULD HAVE A HOBBY

Multinational professional services organisation PwC surveyed 2000 workers in late 2018 about the things they felt they could do to make work more meaningful. They found that employees are 'looking for a work experience that is optimized for meaningful work and personal fulfillment, and encourages a growth mindset and generosity'.[3]

To get there, there are four kinds of shared experiences that mix different levels of meaning and different levels of stress. Hobby activities were identified as low stress, high meaning activities that, when done well, create a medium-level of bonding between teammates. When these activities are deliberately designed, they bring people together and foster a level of belonging. And 82 per cent of those surveyed recognised that finding meaning in their work was their responsibility, while 42 per cent said that they were own their biggest barrier to achieving it.

Sharing each other's hobbies is just one example (there are many more in this book!) of the micro-experiences that organisations can encourage to foster a sense of connectedness.

Not only that, but hobbies can provide personal benefits, too. Research published in *Psychosomatic Medicine* found that engaging in 'multiple enjoyable activities' correlated with lower blood pressure, waist circumference and body mass index; positive psychosocial states; and lower levels of depression.[4]

Additionally, and I can attest to most of these myself, hobbies:

- provide relief from stress and anxiety
- reduce boredom
- help with learning new skills
- provide an opportunity to meet new people
- increase confidence and self-esteem
- provide different perspectives
- increase empathy, and
- distract you from bad habits.

Sometimes you just don't know what will grab your interest until someone introduces you to it, and that's where a hobby expo is a great idea. It provides an opportunity for people to talk about the things that they do in their spare time, and even the chance to demonstrate them.

One of my former colleagues revealed that he played the guitar. He brought it into the office one day and played requests – it was absolutely brilliant and he inspired at least one person (that I know of) to take up the guitar as well. Sometimes all you need is a little inspiration.

A study of 400 employees published in the *Journal of Occupational and Organizational Psychology* found a marked difference in performance between those people who engaged in a hobby and those who didn't. Having a hobby is associated with creativity on projects and also a better attitude on the job.[5]

By far the most popular hobby in many offices is the running club.

RUNNING CLUB

Arthur Leslie Lydiard, ONZ, OBE,[6] was a runner and coach from Auckland, New Zealand. He is considered to be one of the greatest athletic coaches ever, and yet very few people have heard of him. This despite *Runner's World* magazine declaring him to be the 'all-time best running coach'.

His fame in the running world is a result of the performance training systems that he introduced, particularly periodisation. Periodisation exercise programs mix the intensity and volume of work to ensure that an athlete doesn't do too much of either at any one time. Only then can the neuromuscular system – that is, the way that the brain interacts with your body to make it move as you want it to[7] – fully benefit from the exercise.

Training is broken up into 'macrocycles', 'microcycles' and 'meso-cycles', which are long, medium and short periods of exercise.[8]

If you've ever run a marathon, then you will have (probably unwittingly) used a macrocycle where you increase the volume and intensity of your training over four- to six-week periods for a total of 16 to 20 weeks, so that your body is in peak condition prior to running the 26-mile or 42-kilometre track.

This system had been used before, most famously by Sir Roger Bannister,[9] who employed it to become the first person to break the four-minute mile. However, it was Lydiard who perfected it, and periodisation is now used all over the world, including in Ethiopia and Kenya, where athletes excel at long-distance running.

It was also Lydiard who popularised the word 'jogging' in the 1960s, and it was in Auckland that the first documented evidence of a 'jogging club' as an organised activity appeared in a *New Zealand Herald* article in February 1962.[10] University of Oregon coach Bill Bowerman went jogging with Lydiard that year, then returned to the U.S. to form the first jogging club in Eugene, Oregon, in 1963. Over 200 people turned out for the first meeting in February of that year, and it was captured by the Eugene *Register-Guard* newspaper. Bowerman found the turnout 'very gratifying'.[11]

Three years later, in association with cardiologist W.E. Harris, Bowerman wrote and published a book titled *Jogging*, which went on to sell a million copies in the U.S.

A new hobby had been born.

Prior to that, Bowerman had co-founded sports-shoe (now sportswear) company Nike with Phil Knight in 1964 – and the rest, as they say, is history.

In the U.S. alone, it's estimated over 60 million people participated in running in 2017.[12] There are days when I'm cycling around my local park and it feels like there are the same amount of people on the running track!

Opinion is divided as to whether running is good for us, which of course, largely depends on your physiology. As someone with back problems, I can categorically tell you that it's no good for me! The benefits of running include:

- cardiovascular and respiratory health
- weight loss, and
- mental health.

Dis-benefits of running can include:

- impact injuries
- shin splints (the medical name for which is medial tibial stress syndrome), and, of course
- chafing – easily the most painful of all the conditions!

Running clubs have become hugely popular in the corporate world, with many devoting 40 to 60 minutes every day to the activity. They happen before work, during lunch hours or after work. Many teams train together for fun-runs, half-marathons or other charity events. Not only do they encourage high performance, but they help teams with endurance, resilience and accountability. One downside is that runners can bore the pants off you talking about running, but that aside, it's all good.

As you'd expect, Nike provides some excellent insights, not only on how to create your own running club, but also tips on warming up, cooling down and, of course, the equipment you'll need to avoid the rubbing and the chafing.

Regardless of the pastime and whether it's an individual or team exercise, hobbies are highly effective ways for people to stay connected and to build the sense of belonging required for continual cultural evolution.

CULTURE HACK #12:
STRETCH FOR
(POSTURAL) SUCCESS

TL;DR

- Provide advice and support on posture.
- Have a set of stretching exercises that you can use throughout the day.
- Continually refresh your wellness program.

ONE THING TO STOP

- Hunching over your phone or laptop.

In the 2008 Pixar movie *WALL-E*, the writers and director paint a picture of what humans could potentially look like in 700 years' time. In this dystopian world, humans are drifting aimlessly through space in giant ships. They are overweight, unable to walk and being ferried around on electric chairs, in which the occupants eat, drink and mindlessly watch screens nonstop in a world run by a corporation called Buy n Large.

The implied commentary is that, if we carry on as we are with our focus on consumerisation, greed and a devotion to screens – well, things aren't looking great for us. Thirteen years on from the movie and our reliance on screens has only increased further. We spend an average of 5 hours per day browsing[1], check our phones at least 150 times per day[2] and 87 per cent of Millennials say that their phone never leaves their side.[3] A quarter of the people in one survey even said they check their phone when they wake up in the night![4]

Parents are giving devices to children as soon as they're able to support themselves, and it's having an adverse effect on their bodies. Forward head posture (FHP) is becoming a very real problem in teenagers and young adults. The first mention I can find of this research is from 2009, in an article entitled, 'Prevalence of neck pain and headaches: impact of computer use and other associative factors'[5] by Smith, Louw, Crous and Grimmer-Somers. The 1073 students they studied complained of a high prevalence of neck pain and headaches. The researchers 'found a concerning association between neck pain and high hours of computing for school students, and have confirmed the need to educate new computer users (school students) about appropriate ergonomics and postural health'.

A 2019 study confirmed these findings and also found that 'forward head posture causes expansion of the upper thorax and contraction of the lower thorax, and these morphological changes cause decreased respiratory function'.[6]

So in short, hunching over your phone and/or laptop is really bad for you.

The thorax is that bit of your body that goes from the bottom of your neck to the top of your abdomen; among other things, it houses the heart and lungs, which, last time I checked, were pretty important organs for day-to-day human function. You need to look after them.[7]

FHP can lead to:

- neck pain
- back pain
- pins and needles in the arms and hands
- muscle tension in the shoulders
- a reduction in attention, and
- general tiredness.[8]

Do any of those things sound familiar? Are you hunched over this book reading it now? I think I've had all of those symptoms today while writing this, so clearly I have some work to do on my own posture!

FHP (or iHunch[9] as it's been nicknamed) is a real 21st-century problem, especially for those whose jobs involve lots of hunching. Dentists, chefs, nurses and teachers have all suffered the symptoms; however, in the last fifteen years, the number of people affected has increased dramatically.

The good news is that with deliberate action you can retrain your body and undo all of the bad postural habits that you've got yourself into. Providing you want to, of course. As with everything worthwhile, it will take effort and time.

STRETCH OUT AND WAIT

Merriliz Rivera Monzon is a meditation and yoga instructor based in Las Vegas, Nevada. She runs wellness programs for her clients across the U.S., helping people to be more present and more flexible in their day-to-day lives.

There has been much cynicism about the benefits of both yoga and meditation for years, however Monzon now no longer gets this pushback. As she said when I interviewed her, 'People now realise that it's not about sitting on top of a mountain in the middle of the Himalayas!'

Monzon trained – as many have before her – at the O&O Academy, about two hours north of Chennai in south-east India.

The Academy was founded by Sri Preethaji and Sri Krishnaji, who are considered to be two of the most inspirational spiritual leaders in the world today. The academy offers people the chance to 'Transform disconnection to connection, division to oneness, suffering to a beautiful state'. It must work, given the sheer number of people who've attended their courses, and the recommendations from Usher; the former CEO of Patagonia, Casey Sheahan; and the owner of the UFC, Ari Emanuel.

For her part, Monzon has been to India six times to hone her practice and ensure that the wisdom that she passes on to her clients has an immediate impact. Her practice consists of both yoga and meditation.

Yoga originated in ancient India and is one of the six orthodox schools of Hindu philosophical traditions – the others being Sāmkhya (consciousness and matter), Nyāya (sources of knowledge), Vaiśeṣika (atomism), Mīmāṃsā (interpretation of Hindu verses) and Vedānta (knowledge and liberation).[10] Yoga is a mind and body practice. It has a significant number of benefits:

- **Reduced stress** – stress is ever-present in most people's lives and has positive and negative effects on the actions we take. If our brains receive too much cortisol (which is the hormone that causes stress), over time, this can have a negative effect on brain function. Yoga has been proven to reduce cortisol production.

- **Improved posture** – stretching is the most traditional view that people have of yoga, often interpreting it as a game of Twister gone wrong; however, this is a very dated idea. Through careful stretching techniques, yoga has been proven to increase flexibility and reduce joint pain.

- **Increased focus** – the poses and quiet calm of yoga help to clear the mind of thoughts that cloud our judgement and affect our productive time. This in turn helps us to stay focused on the job at hand and alert to anything that may arise.

- **Better digestion** – the improvement in posture ensures that all bodily functions are 'in line' and can take place exactly as they are meant to. Not only that, but yoga improves the rate at which blood flows around our bodies, which not only increases immunity but helps our aches and pains to repair more quickly.

All of these benefits occur at an individual level; when I asked Monzon what benefits yoga generates at a corporate level, she cited increases in:

- productivity
- creativity
- relationships
- decision-making, and
- emotional control.

As part of her programs, Monzon gets her clients to look at the way their offices are set up, to aid wellness: from making the right foods available to snack on, to looking at how the person sits and stands while working. As she says, 'We're not conditioned nor were we meant to sit at a desk eight hours a day. Movement is important to reject the toxins that build up in our bodies'.

Anyone who has ever flown longer than four hours will know how that build-up of toxins makes you feel – which is why most airlines provide written instructions on exercises you should do. They include neck stretches, shoulder rotations, side-to-side turns, arm stretches, calf raises, toe curls and many others. Why not create something similar for the office?

HOW WELL IS YOUR WELLNESS PROGRAM?

Keeping employees healthy is critically important for both parties. In Australia there are some pretty stark figures when it comes to wellness:[11]

- 48 productive working days are lost every year

- 27 per cent slept less than 7 hours a night, and

- 53 per cent have at least one dimension of work-related stress.

Wellness programs are big business now and it's great to see organisations putting thought, time and money into the health and fitness of their employees. After all, if you look after your people, they will look after you.

According to one survey, almost 60 per cent of employees now expect wellness programs as part of their package.[12] This was backed by the 2019 Deloitte Global Millennial survey, which showed that almost 70 per cent would leave their employers if they didn't prioritise the health and wellness of staff.[13] Organisations recognise this and see it as a value-add, to help attract and retain good people, improve engagement and to help with flexible working arrangements. Some great examples include:

- **Microsoft** – not only does it subsidise gym memberships and provide courts for a multitude of sports, it also provides onsite clinics, optometrists and pharmacists, as well as screening services for more serious diseases.

- **Asana** – it provides nap rooms for its employees as well as unlimited leave programs and nutrition programs full of organic produce from local stores. It also holds monthly mentoring workshops to help people with their lifestyle issues.[14]

- **Cisco** – it provides a fun fund, which teams can use to spend on celebrations or activities to bring them closer together. It also has an internal recognition reward where staff can celebrate the achievements of others.

- **Union Pacific** – it takes its wellness mentoring to a different level by helping to save lives. It offers smoking cessation programs and the results have been impressive, with the number of its team that smoke reducing from 40 per cent in the 1990s, to 17 per cent in 2007.[15]

Like most things that don't provide immediate tangible returns, cost is often a concern here, yet the research always shows that organisations get that money back in terms of improved productivity, reduced absenteeism and increased loyalty.

You don't have to build an onsite gym, however: cutting a deal with a local supplier to provide subsidised membership would be a great way to encourage your staff to look after their bodies.

Other things that I've experienced include:

- **Onsite massage** – Zappos in the U.S. does something similar, and when I caught up with the masseur back in 2019, she said that she was booked solid for the next two months!

- **Culinary classes** – where an external chef comes into the office (providing it has a kitchen! – or else you can head to their kitchen) to show staff how to make simple healthy meals.

- **Financial advice** – on more than one occasion (and often before the dreaded tax return was due) an adviser would talk to us about our returns and provide advice on investments we could make.

Whatever you do (and you should be doing something!), you need to ensure that the program remains up-to-date and offers services to employees that can improve the quality of their lives. Take suggestions or else go on a field trip (see Culture Hack #5) to find out what others are doing before figuring out what you have the budget for.

CULTURE HACK #13:
BUST YOUR BUREAUCRACY

TL;DR

- Identify ways of working that don't add value.

- Use a tool to capture ideas.

- Set aside time every month to bust your bureaucracy.

ONE THING TO STOP

- Wasting time and money justifying things to yourselves. There's a certain level of information required to get things started; when you have that, get cracking!

In 2007 we (my wife and one-year-old son) emigrated from the U.K. to New Zealand. I'd been offered a job and we had a second child due in December of that year, so it felt like a great chance for us to change our lives. As part of the transition, I moved from the private sector in the U.K. to a government role in New Zealand.

The organisation I left in the U.K. was in the final stages of a digital transformation program. It had approached the whole program in exactly the right way. It defined the target culture before undertaking the work, involving the staff in the definition process; looked at ways it could strip out inefficient workflows in order to streamline operations; held management accountable to project milestones; and actively managed out those who attempted to get in the way of progress through their behaviours or their performance. It was a joy to be part of.

It turns out that the government machine doesn't work in quite the same way.

Don't get me wrong: the people and the organisation that I went to work for in New Zealand were absolutely fantastic and we couldn't have been made to feel more welcome. However, it was quite a culture shock moving from an organisation that cut out inefficient work and continually challenged poor behaviour to one that, well, didn't do any of those things, because, you know, government.

I understood the need for justification when spending public money, but providing about a dozen presentations on the justification, then re-justifying it to a different set of people, only to be told we were justifying the wrong thing, I didn't understand. Oh, and then to be told that it was no longer a priority, when we felt we'd finally got the justification over the line, I understood even less.

Thankfully, one of my tasks was to take complexity out of the way that we did things and it was a task I undertook with relish. And yet, there seemed to be an endless line of people ready to tell me that the changes I was proposing couldn't be done, often before they'd even heard what they were.

I joke on stage that nobody wants to come to work to be the worst version of themselves and that people don't deliberately get in the way of progress, but honestly, there were days…

A lot of it has to do with the confusing nature of the government sector. Often things are done on the whim of a minister and everyone is expected to jump through a different set of hoops than they are used to. It isn't so much rule-breaking as process avoidance (note: they now call this 'being agile'). Or else, someone has always done something a particular way and now sees it as a comfort blanket: something that can protect them until such time as they reach retirement age and can pack up their folders, stapler and hole punch and see out their days at the beach house.

When I challenged unnecessary process, I frequently heard sayings such as:

- 'That's the policy.'
- 'That's the way it's always been done.'
- 'I'll need authority from [insert senior manager's name] to change this.'
- '[Government minister's name] insists on [insert name of pointless document].'

My question was always, 'What's the value of us doing this, in this way, to our customers?' A simple question, but often one that people hadn't thought about, because 'That's the way it's always been done'.

BUREAUCRACY KILLS AGILITY

Writing in *Forbes* magazine in 2019, Steve Denning outlined the three laws of being agile:[1]

1. the law of the customer
2. the law of the small team
3. the law of the network.

The law of the customer involves an organisation being obsessed with delivery of value to the customer. That requires a full understanding of their needs and being clear on how they'll be involved in the delivery of the products or services that will provide that value.

The law of the small team recognises that in order to deliver value quickly to the customer, short work cycles that use fewer people are the way to get things done. In these teams, the individuals organise themselves, rotate the ownership of tasks and focus on the incremental delivery of value.

The law of the network, meanwhile, is the continual effort to strip away hierarchy, bureaucracy and anything else that gets in the way of a network of smaller teams delivering the expected value to the customer. Handovers are minimised and people are empowered to make decisions. Without this law, neither of the former two are possible, because the law of the network often challenges the very fabric of an organisation.

Many attempts to be more agile in the way that products are delivered fail because senior managers try to apply the veneer of a shiny new method to wood that has already rotted. Command and control structures – where people are promoted based on length of tenure, not leadership skills – are employed to ensure that everyone knows what they should be doing and who to approach to get a decision.

These combatant cultures overpromise, underdeliver and love to create endless committees and working groups, cultivating as much complexity as they can. Then they wonder why they're not able to take an idea, develop it quickly and continually iterate it until the customer value is delivered. It has nothing to do with the methods being employed and everything to do with the mindsets of the people who refuse to address the bureaucracy holding them back.

Once you start to address these things – and it was something I made a habit of in the eight years that I spent working in government – a magical thing happens. People become less reliant on process, make decisions themselves, interact more regularly with customers and rely less on overly formal meetings in which every breath must be minuted.

And all of this (often) needless activity costs money. According to one report in the U.S., it adds up to almost $3 trillion per year, as a result of too many managers, not enough workers, too much work that gets in the way of decisions, too many impediments to proactive change and too much energy devoted to gaining power and influence.[2]

BUSTING MAKES YOU FEEL GOOD

I heard many managers in government telling people that 'We ought to be thinking like a start-up', when the reality was, their cultures were the antithesis of that. There was no way that any new venture would have accepted the level of indecision or waste they had, or would have carried so many passengers within the culture.

Ron Jeffries was an original signatory of the Agile Manifesto (see Culture Hack #16) and in a 2018 blog post he was scathing about organisations implementing (his words) 'so-called agile approaches', rather than placing faith in their people to figure out the right way to do things, and not overburdening them with unnecessary policy and process. He said, 'The Manifesto calls for "self-organizing" teams, and in the best case, that comes down to the team choosing its own process. If I were starting a company, I'd let the teams choose any process they wish'.[3]

Great cultures (and this is not limited to start-ups or technology organisations) never stop looking for ways to enhance the value that they add, by removing layers of unnecessary activity and ensuring that their people understand that they're empowered to do so. The benefits of this approach are:

- the ability to pivot or reprioritise quickly
- the creation of a culture of continual improvement
- people working smarter, not harder
- increased trust and empowerment
- better decision-making
- improved retention of key staff, and
- faster delivery of value.

Sometimes, of course, the people who get in the way of busting the bureaucracy need to be removed, and vibrant workplace cultures recognise this and do it well.

Ray Dalio talks about this in *Principles*, specifically in relation to the governance provided by senior managers at Bridgewater Associates. He says, 'Governance is the oversight system that removes the people and the processes if they aren't working well'. People and processes, in that order.

Back in 2009, Google was expanding, diversifying its offerings and looking to speed up its search engine so that it remained the number-one tool for finding content on the web. More people joined and greater control was given to teams. While this was a good thing, the leadership team wanted to ensure that the expanded organisation retained its commitment to lean, efficient ways of working. So, Patrick Pichette, then Senior Vice President and Chief Financial Officer, established an initiative called Bureaucracy Busters. This biannual program was an opportunity for Googlers to come together to identify the biggest barriers to getting productive work done or their biggest frustrations with the way things worked, and provided them with the opportunity to discuss and address these.

At the first Bureaucracy Busters, 570 ideas were generated and voted on over 55,000 times, and most of the issues were tiny things that could be easily resolved. The teams were empowered to go and do so.[4]

This is a tactic that can be copied by any culture, anywhere. It doesn't have to be biannual; it can be monthly or weekly, and it can be done at a team, department or organisation level – whatever works within the context of what you do. It may require you to teach your people *how* to look for inefficient process, rather than to just blindly follow it, but it's an investment that's worth making.

The key aim of bureaucracy busting has to be to deliver value more quickly, through simplification. You could also do what organisations such as Syngenta have done and create a Chief Simplification Officer role to hold everyone to account.

Now, before you start with your 'They never had one of those in my day' or 'What will HR think of next?' comments, I think this role should be independent, report directly to the CEO and continually highlight areas of value-loss, to ensure that the organisation remains match-fit for whatever the future may throw at it.

Failing that, you could create a Simplicity Circle: a small group of people who bring the inefficiencies from their areas together and vote on what to address first. This means that the senior management team needs to be committed to not only supporting continual improvement, but also providing time and money to help eradicate the things holding them back.

In my eight years in government, I'm proud to say that the teams I was part of were able to get rid of so much unnecessary paperwork that people wondered how some of it became part of the process in the first place. However, without continual challenge, it's possible that those inefficiencies will return, with a different name and on a different swim-lane diagram. Regular bureaucracy busting can help ensure that never happens.

CULTURE HACK #14:
BREAK OUT
THE BOARD GAMES

TL;DR

- Raid your local charity shops for team games.
- Mix longer and shorter games at various stages of the day.
- Create a league table to encourage healthy competition.

ONE THING TO STOP

- Taking board games too seriously! They're supposed to be fun.

Boxing Day was always my favourite part of Christmas when I was growing up in Liverpool. Don't get me wrong, I loved the presents and the huge dinner that Mum made on Christmas Day, but there was just something about Boxing Day that I can never replicate with my own family.

The day went something like this: breakfast, play with presents, chocolate, leftover lunch, trip to Goodison Park (to watch Everton if they were at home; otherwise, we'd listen to the game on the radio), quick snack, change and get ready and wait with anticipation for the relatives to arrive and the games to start.

The entire day could be a disaster – not enough leftovers, pouring with rain, freezing cold, Everton loss – but it would all be rectified in that last five to eight hours (depending on people's stamina and possible fallouts).

The history of parlour games in England goes back – like most things do – hundreds of years. In 877 A.D., Alfred the Great created a law that granted all servants twelve days of holidays following Christmas Day. The church was not in favour and warned their flock against 'frivolous speech, board games and drinking parties'. No Cards Against Humanity for these guys then![1] It's a tradition that stuck.

That's not to say that the board game originated in England. It very probably originated in the Middle East. According to Wikipedia, the oldest board game known to have existed is called Senet and has been found in burial sites in Egypt dating from 3500 B.C.[2] The exact rules of Senet aren't fully known or understood, but it has 30 squares in three rows of ten, some of which have pictures on them which are thought to represent good and bad luck. The winner was the first person to pass into the afterlife, which was achieved by getting all their pieces off the board.[3]

It was played by royalty, too. Queen Nefertari (wife of Ramesses II) is pictured playing it in her tomb, as it was meant to ward off evil spirits.[4]

The board games played on Boxing Day in our house seemed to increase the chances of evil spirits appearing, as a result of all the alcoholic spirits being drunk. Now of course, you don't need to drink to enjoy a game – although Twister is rubbish without it. It's like doing inappropriate yoga with a bunch of friends and no-one wants to do that by choice. Some (if not most) games, however, are best played with a clear head. Chess is one of them.

CHECK, MATE

Chess is thought to have been derived from an Indian game called *chaturanga* sometime prior to the 7th century, or from the ancient Chinese game *xiangqi*, depending on which back story you believe.[5] The pieces bore no resemblance to those that Ron Weasley played in Wizard Chess in J.K. Rowling's 1997 book *Harry Potter and the Philosopher's Stone*. They only assumed their current form in Spain in the late 15th century, and the rules that are used to play chess today were standardised in the 19th century.[6]

Chess is number one in the top ten board games of all time,[7] in one of those lists designed only to cause rancour and disagreement and reprinted here to do the very same. In order they are:

1. Chess

2. Checkers

3. Backgammon

4. Scrabble

5. Monopoly

6. Clue/Cluedo

7. Othello

8. Trivial Pursuit

9. Pictionary, and

10. Risk.

Chess is a game that requires skill and patience, which is why I avoid it. There are over 47 different opening moves, including things like Bird's Opening, Elephant Gambit, Torre Attack and French Defence. To me, French Defence is something that contains Lilian Thuram, Sandrine Soubeyrand or Lucas Digne, and has nothing to do with moving a pawn forward one space.

It's dangerous, too. At the 41st Chess Olympiad, deep in the Arctic Circle in Tromsø, Norway in 2014, two players died within hours of each other.[8]

And 1973–75 was dominated by the rivalry between Anatoly Karpov and Bobby Fischer, who played matches that were watched by millions of people around the world. I can't imagine my kids sitting down and watching a chess match, but apparently it happened. Indeed, Fischer was credited with modernising the game by researching, testing and preparing different openings.

During the COVID-19 crisis I was talking to my friend Carl in Jacksonsville, Florida, prior to doing a keynote for his digital community, and I asked him what positives he'd found while being isolated. He told me a story about how he and one of his friends had rigged up a chess board so that they could play each other via video call. He said it was the thing that he looked forward to most about his day.

Another friend told me a similar story, but this time involving Dungeons & Dragons (D&D). In the mid-1970s and for about ten years after that, D&D was huge. According to one article, in 2004 it was estimated that over 20 million people had played it – and that was before the Netflix show *Stranger Things* reignited its popularity in 2016. Now that estimate is close to 40 million.[9]

In short – if you're not one of the 40 million – it was the first real role-playing game that involved all manner of adventures. Each game had an umpire/storyteller known at the Dungeon Master. It's a co-operative game that is played around an actual board, rather than digitally, which is part of its appeal. The senior art director for D&D, Richard Whitters, commented, '[Being around a central structure] is a thing that humans have always done: gathering around the campfire, telling stories, interacting. And for many players, D&D is an event'.[10]

COVID-19 provided teams (and families) around the world with the opportunity to be creative about the ways they socialised together, given that they weren't spending time together in their usual ways, and D&D was a game that people returned to. It allows players to explore different characters and sides to their personalities, while getting to know the other players better.

ENGAGED, NOT 'BOARD'

Board games are a great way to bring people together, especially in an age when most social activities seem to centre around the things that extroverts love doing, such as karaoke, bowling and drinking. Once you've made the initial outlay on games, they can provide payback for years.

You don't even have to buy new copies of games. I once sent a team that I was working with out to buy one board game per person. I gave them $10 each and they had to scour the charity shops (thrift stores), find the best game they could and bring it back for everyone to play.

One team brought back Buckaroo, which was the source of much amusement during breaks over the remainder of our two days together. Another group bought the game Pass the Bomb, and to my knowledge they still play it now.

In my experience, and having played board games in work for many years, they're a fantastic way to generate conversation, healthy competition and co-operation, and to create shared stories (on which great cultures are built) in the process.

You can even create league ladders to keep track of who's beating who, then have a celebration and a trophy at the end of the year, but it's not necessary, of course. The focus should be on the benefits that playing board games provides, for both individuals and teams. These include:[11]

- **Stress reduction** – they're a great way to switch off stress or anxiety for 15 to 30 minutes and focus on something not related to the tasks at hand. According to RealNetworks Inc., 53 per cent of people surveyed played games to reduce their stress.[12]

- **Fun** – fun is something that can't be forced and, of course, we all have different ideas of what 'fun' actually is. When it comes to board games, chess is no fun for me, but Operation most definitely is. So, forcing people to play particular board games is a way of potentially alienating people and increasing stress! That's why there have to be multiple types of games that people can engage in. When people are having fun, there's laughter, and where there's laughter, there's reduced blood pressure, an immune system boost, calorie burning and relief of physical tension – and who doesn't want all of that?!

- **Cognitive skills** – that's right, games are good for the brain, too, specifically the prefrontal cortex and the hippocampus. Those are the bits that are responsible for complex thought and memory function. Games like Simon definitely push the brain to its limits, while Guess Who? and Battleships at least provide us with mechanisms to aid our memory.

- **Relationship-building** – you don't really know a person until you've played them at Trivial Pursuit. That mild-mannered accountant who you barely talked to suddenly becomes a hyper-competitive, strategic, picky bugger who insists that the answer has to match what's on the card exactly. You know the type, right? But seriously, games are a fantastic way to build connection between people and also add to the sense of belonging within a team.

- **Culture enhancement** – of course, games add to the uniqueness of a culture, which is obviously why this Culture Hack is in the book. One idea is to form an Uno club (or similar) and create a championship to compete for, with the winner getting a crappy trophy at the end. If other departments get wind of it, they will want in – instead, encourage them to create their own league and have play-offs for an ultimate championship.

You might find out about someone's passion for a particular game through your hobby-sharing (see Culture Hack #11), so don't miss the opportunity to encourage them to bring the game in. We had a box in the kitchen where we kept our board games and people would play them during breaks, lunchtimes and so on. People even left the office late if they were in the middle of Game of Life.

Often, what gets in the way of this happening is a lack of trust from management – a perception that people are somehow wasting time, when the opposite is true. When people take time to build connection, it adds to the vibrancy of a culture and increases productivity. Obviously, if targets are being missed that's a different story and needs to be managed, but it's never been an issue in the teams that I was part of, because we recognised the importance of taking a break from what we did to recharge our cognitive batteries.

By having a few games that can be played in the office when people need a break, you can ensure that they take time away from their screens and are never 'board'.

CULTURE HACK #15:
START A PODCAST

TL;DR

- Share your stories internally and externally.
- Improve understanding of the way you do things.
- Provide a platform to 'sell' your culture.

ONE THING TO STOP

- Thinking that it's hard to start a podcast – it's not.

Michael Barbaro joined *The Washington Post* as a journalist in 2002. Three years later, he joined *The New York Times* as a business journalist and covered Walmart, New York City Hall and the American retail industry. However, Barbaro came to prominence in 2016 while he was covering the 2016 U.S. presidential campaign, and in particular, 'outsider' Donald Trump.

With three months to go and as the campaigns of Trump and Hillary Clinton reached fever pitch, *The New York Times* decided to do something different. It launched a podcast to cover the final three months of the election. The podcast was called *The Run-Up* and Barbaro was appointed to be its host, given his knowledge of the candidates and their campaigns.

The twice-a-week show promised to 'make sense of a campaign that has baffled, shocked and reordered the political world'. I'll be honest, I'm not sure they did that![1]

Barbaro was almost immediately at ease in the chair and the *Times* realised that it was onto something. So at the beginning of 2017, with the election over, it launched a daily podcast and called it, simply, *The Daily.* The aim of *The Daily* is to cover all the major news stories of the day in 20 to 25 minutes; almost immediately it was a success. In 2018, *The Daily* occupied either the number one or two spot on the U.S. podcast charts, and in 2019 it was the number-one podcast every single month. With the level of news as I write this book in 2020, I can't see it being replaced any time soon.

It's recorded in a back office of the *Times'* headquarters on Eighth Avenue in New York every day, and has made Barbaro a household name. The influence of the show continues to grow at pace.

For *The New York Times*, it has provided access to an audience that prior to August 2016 was inconceivable. Over two million people download the show, compared with around 440,000 who read the printed version of the paper.[2]

As you'd expect, rival publishers have now started their own podcasts, because, well, it's not that hard to do.

IPOD, THEREFORE I AM

So where did this phenomenon come from? Well, it all started with the release of the iPod in 2001 – but you probably already guessed that.

It's hard for anyone under the age of 25 to come to terms with the fact that before 2001 it just wasn't possible to have all of your favourite music available to you all the time. We bought vinyl records and played them on gramophones until the late 1970s, at which point the compact cassette arrived. We recorded our vinyl records onto blank tapes or else we just bought the album on cassette so that we could listen to our music on our Sony Walkmans (or cheaper, more shit alternatives).

By the mid-1980s, compact discs (CDs) were added to this mix, and by 1988 sales of vinyl and tapes plummeted as we invested in CDs and CD players – but it was still only one album at a time. If we wanted to listen to more than one album (on holiday, say, or on public transport), then we had to invest in a PVC case with a zip around the outside that had spaces to slide in 48 CDs (but not their boxes). One of the biggest stresses of my life was when I thought I'd lost my CD case, and with it my Smiths, INXS, Beautiful South, Doors and Stone Roses CDs (to name just a few). I eventually found it under the car seat.

Apple changed everything forever in 2001 with the release of the first-generation iPod. By the time I bought my first iPod (a third generation model at the end of 2003, which I still have some-where), the audio transformation was in full swing. CDs were being burned to PCs and then iTunes was used to catalogue the tracks and add them to the iPod: it was genius. It did give rise to significant piracy issues (which continue to affect artists to this day), but provided listeners with a choice that they'd never had before.

By 2004, people were looking at different ways to import audio other than music onto their iPods. Former MTV video jockey (remember those?) Adam Curry was one such person.

Back in 2004 – so the story goes – Curry wrote a program that he called iPodder, which enabled him to download his favou-rite radio stations onto his iPod. Curry had taken inspiration from the AppleScript code of software developer Dave Winer and the two are now credited with the creation of podcasts, which were then called 'audio enclosures'. Thankfully that name didn't stick![3, 4]

What continues to be unique about podcasts is that they are free from regulation. No licences are required and no regulations have to be followed; anything goes. However, copyright law does apply, so it's a win-win for podcasters.

According to one survey from Edison Research[5] in 2020, podcasts now reach over 100 million Americans alone every month! Seventy-five per cent of people aged twelve-plus are familiar with podcasting and 37 per cent (104 million people) listen to them every month.

When I did an online search for 'podcast' while researching this book, it returned over one billion results. Compare this to 16 years ago. On 28 September 2004, Doc Searls, a blogger and technology columnist and commentator, began recording how many search results were returned for the word 'podcast'. On that day in 2004 it was 24.

The growth in smart speaker ownership will only provide further opportunities for podcasts to have an impact on our home lives. It's estimated that an average of 2.2 smart speaker devices are owned per household, as opposed to 1.7 just two years ago. My Dad's generation grew up learning new things and listening to stories and serials on the radio – it looks like we're going to come full circle and do that all again. Everything old will become new again, as they say. Except tartan trousers. Surely we've seen the last of them?

The thing about podcasting is that it's really not that hard to do. I'm a podcaster myself and honestly couldn't believe how simple it was to get started. In fact, the hardest part of my *Culture Makers* podcast (anchor.fm/culturemakers) is getting people to appear on the show. (So, if you're in business and have a great culture story to share, get in touch!)

One of my favourite podcasters is Gary Vaynerchuk, who also happens to be great at sharing how he gets things done. An avid new-media advocate, Vaynerchuk has been encouraging brands to start podcasts for the last few years, and in 2019 his podcast engineer Seth Feingersh produced a fantastic list of equipment to buy at kit.co/sethfeingersh. He covers everything from budget to high quality, mobile to home studio.

I wanted something that I could take with me on my travels as well as set up and record via video-conferencing at home. I purchased a Zoom H6 portable recording unit, two microphones and cables, two microphone shields to reduce the air pressure when speaking, a cable to run from my laptop audio to the Zoom and an SD card to capture my recordings.

We set up an account with Anchor (anchor.fm), which pretty much does every single thing for you, including distributing your podcast to other platforms such as Apple Podcasts and Spotify. Anchor also provides a whole heap of tutorials and tips to help you improve.

GET RECORDING

Of course, just because you can start a podcast doesn't mean you should; however, as a business or team, you have many different stories to share internally and externally about the way you do things, and a podcast could have the following benefits:

- **Accessibility** – podcasting gives you an opportunity to share things about your culture that makes you more accessible either to your staff or your customers. This, in turn, will help build an audience of people who are keen to know more about you or the way that you do things.

- **Reputation** – podcasting provides you with the opportunity to boost your reputation or increase brand awareness. General Electric, McDonald's, Sephora, eBay, Basecamp and Johnson & Johnson are just a small sample of organisations who have done just that.

- **Revenue** – this is probably not high on the list of reasons for starting a podcast for businesses; however, as *The New York Times* has shown, there is an opportunity to gain sponsorship or advertising revenue through your podcast.

- **Humanity** – sharing stories of the way that you do things or asking people within the organisation to be a little bit vulnerable helps people to see the humanity of the organisation. This has to be handled with care, of course.

- **It's fun** – well, if you do it right, it definitely can be! You could focus on the lighter side of things within your culture or else interview people with funny stories to tell.

- **Attraction** – of course, it's the perfect way to get people interested in joining you. You don't have to produce a hipster podcast, just something in line with your values that demonstrates the human side of the organisation and its continued relevance within today's content-hungry world.

Once you've captured why you should do a podcast, then you have to plan how you're going to do it – and you want to plan for the long term, not the short term. If you plan for the latter, then you'll lose steam early on and the weekly podcast will become monthly, then bimonthly and probably then dropped altogether, with people wondering what happened to it.

When I started my podcast, I had a good look (and listen) to everything in the market and chose a topic that was in line with the work that I do, and also guests who I felt could add value to my listeners, and the feedback so far has been great. When it comes to your topic, you can pretty much pick anything. There are podcasts on diverse subjects such as carp fishing, quilt making, funeral directing, penny loafers, roofing, pencils and dentistry. I even appeared on a dentistry podcast myself last year and it was lots of fun!

Decide on a timing that will suit the audience that you're looking for. Who are the people that will listen to your podcast? How much time are they likely to have on their hands? When will they listen to it? How much time do you have to record the content? Who will be your first few guests and how will you prepare them for the recording? How many people will it be run by?

The recording of the podcast is easy compared to the planning and the lining up of guests; however, you definitely shouldn't let this stop you from getting your thoughts out into the world.

As many organisations have found, starting a podcast has been a fantastic way to engage staff and customers alike, and with listeners increasing, the question isn't 'Why would we start one?' it's 'Why wouldn't we start one?'

CULTURE HACK #16:
HOLD A SHOWCASE

TL;DR

- Create a ceremony to show others what you're working on.

- Hold a monthly event to showcase what a department does.

- Have regular brown-bag lunches to introduce something new.

ONE THING TO STOP

- Technical presentations that do nothing but confuse.
  Think about what the audience wants to see and hear.

In the late 1990s, the biggest thing everyone had to worry about was not what to wear to the party on 31 December 1999, but whether the world as we knew it would still exist in the year 2000.

Many of the technical systems that had been implemented during the preceding fifteen years only held the year (in their memory) as two digits; so, '1999' would just be '99'. The fear was that when we ticked over to the year 2000 (Y2K), this would simply reset to '00', causing internal programming to assume it was 1900 not 2000, and leading to systems around the world catastrophically failing. There was also a secondary issue around the Gregorian calendar, which I never understood, but the consequences of this were considered just as dire.[1] In a nutshell, lots of clever people seemed to be very worried. As a human race we did what we normally do in these situations: we listened intently, but before they finished talking we pressed the panic button.

Thinking back now, the level of hysteria surrounding the 'Millennium Bug' seems incredible. Of course, the problem was real, but the impacts being predicted seem ludicrous. Planes were going to fall from the sky, nuclear missile systems were going to launch themselves, power plants were going to fail, looting would be widespread, and we'd essentially go back to the dark ages.

You know things look bad when *The Simpsons* produces an episode parodying the events, which they did in 'Treehouse of Horror X' in a segment called 'Life's a glitch, then you die'. Homer is the nuclear power plant's Y2K co-ordinator. You can imagine the rest.

The world came together and created a kind of super task force, with every organisation appointing someone (the aforementioned Y2K co-ordinator) to ensure that systems did what they should on 1 January 2000.

In 1997, I was selling advertising space to pubs and clubs in Liverpool for the regional newspaper, the *Liverpool Echo*. I didn't much enjoying selling, but I loved three things about the job:

1. The pub and club owners knew me when I went out in the city on Friday and Saturday nights, which was always good for a free drink.

2. I was working in close proximity to the people who reported on Everton (my football team), so I could be at the cutting edge of team and transfer news (and tickets to big away games).

3. I was an active member of a great team.

It was the latter and the impending Y2K that provided me with an opportunity that changed my life.

The newspaper's advertising, sales and editorial computer systems all used two-digit years and therefore had to be changed. The group decided to establish a team to manage the changes required at all of their newspapers around the country, and went on the hunt for good people.

When that hunt ended and they still had gaps, they asked me whether I'd like to become a project manager. I didn't have a clue what a project manager was, let alone anything to do with IT, but was assured that I would get a car, phone and laptop, be away from home and living in hotels around the U.K. for four years, and would get a bonus at the end if everything went well. I accepted. (I'd always wanted a job that gave me a car.)

There was lots to be done in less than three years, but I loved every minute of the work that we did and we achieved our goal with days to spare. We collected our bonuses and celebrated the continuation of the world, along with everyone else, on 1 January 2000. Worldwide spend on Y2K was over $450 billion.[2] In hindsight, people said it had been a hoax or an overreaction, but those of us who worked on it know that we saved the world from oblivion. You're all welcome.

COMMAND AND CONTROL NO MORE

At the time of the Y2K crisis, empathy for software developers and infrastructure engineers was low. Command and control structures, so prevalent in the 70s and 80s, returned (if they ever went away) and heavy demands were placed on the people of whom so much was expected.

Post-Y2K, the situation didn't get any better. We'd moved into a new, technology-dependent world and managers saw the opportunity to further enhance the way that systems were used to streamline their businesses and save money. By 2001, a group of people had had enough.

Between 11 and 13 February, seventeen software developers met at a ski resort in Utah to talk through the issues that they'd seen and find some common ground on which they could all agree. They were all 'organisational anarchists' and wanted to challenge the lack of humanity that they now saw in the businesses they worked for. These businesses had become process-heavy and demanded huge piles of documentation for every single initiative that was being undertaken, rather than empowering and trusting people to use their expertise to get the job done in the way they saw fit.

The output from the three days was the Agile Manifesto: four values and twelve principles designed to transform the way organisations delivered products to their customers.[3] One key element of the manifesto, which is continually overlooked in my opinion, is that it was designed to put trust and empowerment back into workplace cultures. This is my favourite part of the Manifesto:

> *It's about delivering good products to customers by operating in an environment that does more than talk about 'people as our most important asset' but actually 'acts' as if people were the most important.*

The four values that the team defined were:

1. Individuals and interactions over processes and tools.

2. Working software over comprehensive documentation.

3. Customer collaboration over contract negotiation.

4. Responding to change over following a plan.

Great working cultures around the world do all of these things without ever having to 'go agile', because they recognise the quality of the people they've hired and want to create conditions in which they're able to do their best work. All of which – by happy coincidence – conforms to these values. For command-and-control organisations, embracing these values is much harder, and they resort to rolling out a training course in the hope that that works instead. It never does.

Agility requires a different mindset from managers and employees alike – a mindset that embraces uncertainty, but that still has a good plan for collaborating to deliver working products as quickly as possible.

SHOWCASE TO IMPRESS

A big part of the agile process is presenting what has been produced at regular intervals, to ensure that it's in line with the customer's expectations. These are called 'iteration' or 'sprint' reviews. These reviews are an opportunity to demonstrate, reflect, assess, discuss and get feedback on what's been built so that the next phase (or sprint) can begin. The team should be able to fully demonstrate what they've built at this point and it should match what was promised at the start of the sprint, to keep progress on track.

These presentations are called 'showcases' and their purpose is threefold:

1. demonstrate the work that's been completed

2. gather facts on how the product works, and

3. highlight any potential risks or issues.

The benefits of working in this way include:

- immediate feedback
- different insights from different stakeholders
- cross-organisation collaboration
- visible failure and learning (see Culture Hack #9), and
- a chance for celebration of work completed.

Of course, showcases aren't things that can be 'done on the fly': they have to be well-planned events. They can be formal or informal, take place at a particular time of day on a given week (or not!), delivered in a presentation space or be around some-one's desk, and/or utilise video conferencing or collaboration tools. At a minimum, the showcase should include:

- an overview of the 'problem' being solved over the preceding time period
- an introduction to the team that worked on it
- some context of the overall project and the link to the organisation's vision
- progress to date
- the demonstration itself
- possible risks or issues identified
- feedback from users
- an overview of what's to be covered in the next development period, and
- gratitude and thanks.

Like all good gatherings, it should have an agenda (if you're tak-ing the more formal route) that's circulated in advance, an owner to manage proceedings, a well-prepared presentation that's practised in advance of the session, some ground rules and a way of accurately capturing feedback.[4, 5, 6, 7]

In my experience and like most things, showcases often don't go to plan, so it's important to prepare for surprises or else have some responses prepared it everything fails. I think vulnerability and honesty work best in these scenarios, as we've all had times when we think, 'I have absolutely no idea why that's happened!'

Once the showcase is finished, the team working on the product should come back together to review the feedback and not only assess what needs to change (if anything) for the next sprint, but also look at how they've worked as a team and whether they need to make any changes to this. I actively encourage teams to do this in the organisations I work with, as I want them to be comfortable with feedback – and also to continually create the conditions in which great work can flourish.

There's a danger that some organisations might see these 'ceremonies' as something that can only be used in the software development world, yet they've actually been around for years now – just not with the structures that we currently see. The 'brown-bag lunch' ('BBL' for brevity's sake) in particular is something that I took part in back in the U.K. in the early 2000s, and something that I really enjoyed. It's so named because it originally referred to people bringing their lunch from home, in a brown bag. It's a term that we still use because 'sushi-in-an-environmentally-responsible-container lunch' is a bit of a mouthful, in more ways than one.

A BBL provides an informal opportunity for continual learning or sharing of ideas during a break. They work best when there is a short presentation and then an opportunity for discussion, followed by another short presentation that provides some impetus for action.

As a professional speaker, it's something that I'm asked to do a lot and something that I thoroughly enjoy. I like the social, informal nature of them. They often take place in a large meeting space or dining area and have a completely different energy than a more formal training program.

I run monthly leadership programs for two clients in exactly this way. One takes place in a kitchen over breakfast; the other happens over coffee and biscuits in a large communal space in the afternoon. There are well attended, as people see them as a break from the norm and also a more informal way to learn from and interact with others within the organisation who they wouldn't ordinarily get the opportunity to speak to.

As part of these sessions, I encourage people from different departments to showcase the things that they're working on and their successes. It can also be good for teams to provide some information on who they are, the work they do and their role in supporting others to achieve success.

Showcases are a great way to bring people together. You could have a different department present each month, have a theme and even get creative around presentation styles – anything at all that can add value to the people that you invite and demonstrate that people are the most important thing.

CULTURE HACK #17:
WRITE A WHITE PAPER

TL;DR

- Move to a minimum viable documentation model.
- Crowdsource for ideas.
- Be creative around the way you present your ideas.

ONE THING TO STOP

- Writing boring reports and presenting in 'standard' PowerPoint templates.

During the Crusades, the town of Jaffa, in the Mediterranean basin, found itself in the middle of a couple of skirmishes. King Richard I himself led an army that captured the town in 1191. However, by the 19th century, things had been quiet for the best part of 200 years. Then all that changed: Jaffa went from quiet town to bustling port and became an important gateway for pilgrims heading to Jerusalem.[1]

Tel Aviv (now capital of Israel) grew out of the suburbs of the mainly Arab Jaffa in the 20th century, and there were tensions between the two areas – particularly with regards to the British rule over the area. At the end of 1917, Britain had 'conquered' Palestine and ruled the area until the establishment of a civil administration on 1 July 1920. During this British Mandate era, two different social systems evolved: one Jewish and one Arab. Exchanges between the two groups were commonplace and on 1 May 1921, a violent, bloody conflict exploded which led to the death of 47 Jews and 48 Arabs.[2]

An investigative commission was undertaken by the British, yet the report published on 1 October 1921 was deemed inadequate by both sides. So, with tensions continuing to mount, a further paper was commissioned by then Secretary of State for the Colonies, Winston Churchill.

Winston Leonard Spencer Churchill,[3] born in Blenheim, Oxfordshire in England in 1874, was in 1921 considered to be a man of great potential in David Lloyd George's liberal government. Before he became Secretary of State for the Colonies, he was Secretary of State for War and Air and was responsible for demobilising the army after World War I.

Churchill wanted to resolve the Palestine situation and sought to put together a policy that catered to both parties. It was intended to reinforce the Balfour Declaration[4] (which supported the establishment of a 'national home for the Jewish people' in Palestine), while also providing Arabs with the assurance that Palestine would not become a Jewish state where Arabs would be considered inferior.

It was hoped that the paper would provide clarity for all and re-establish a peaceful equilibrium in the area. In the end, it achieved neither and merely brought more anger to an already inflamed situation. It did, however, achieve something else. It became the best-known example of a 'white paper', a term which originated with the British.

A 'green paper' (yes, printed on green paper) is an in-house document written by government personnel (or 'civil servants' as they're known in England) and presents an idea or topic for consultation. A 'white paper' is also named for the colour of the paper it is printed on, which highlights that the document is for public consumption.

Green papers are a way for government to present an idea to its stakeholders or the general public to gauge their response; after this, a white paper is written and published.[5] A white paper is defined as 'an authoritative report or guide that informs readers concisely about a complex issue and presents the issuing body's philosophy on the matter. It is meant to help readers understand an issue, solve a problem, or make a decision'.[6]

Since the mid-1990s, the term 'white paper' has been appropriated by businesses and individuals around the world. White papers are a powerful tool for marketers and content producers to position themselves or their organisation as an authority on a topic or to present research that reinforces the need for their products or services.[7]

Having written a couple of white papers myself, I can tell you that the hardest part is getting started. The process of selecting an idea that you wish to put out into the world is daunting, as you want it to be well received and start a conversation.

In 2018, I published a white paper called 'Project Delivery – What Next?: 5 Recommendations on how to evolve the business of getting things delivered' (you can download it from colindellis. com/white-papers). With projects continuing to fail at alarming rates around the world, my aim was to challenge how people traditionally think about project management and provide some predictions on how the world of delivery may change.

These ideas were based on the things that I'd seen work in my permanent jobs, the research that I'd undertaken – principally around the importance of emotional intelligence and culture definition – and the conversations that I'd had with others.

But getting started was a nightmare. Seriously, I can write a 55,000-word book faster than I can write a 7500-word white paper! In hindsight, I overthought the process of writing it, eschewing my usual 'published not perfect' approach for over-cautiousness, and worrying too much about how the ideas would be received. As it was, the feedback was positive, and I was asked to present the ideas at many conferences that year. Not everyone agreed with my recommendations – but then, it would be a dull world if everyone agreed with everyone all the time.

WHY BE BEIGE WHEN YOU CAN BE WHITE?

Why would you write a white paper and distribute it internally or externally? Put simply, lots of people have lots of ideas that could make a real difference to the way that you do things. So instead of pushing everyone through a complex business-case-building process, why not be more creative and write a white paper instead?

When I worked in government in New Zealand, the people who oversaw the approval of projects introduced a three-stage business-case process to ensure that the justification for projects was sound. It's not that the process for checking the justification was wrong, it's just that it was so utterly unimaginative, when a simpler approach could have achieved the same output. A white paper could most definitely have been used at this early stage.

However, many organisations love their endless, pointless, boring reports too much to ever consider doing anything any different. I can't tell you how many of these things I've had to read, and while I accept that as a senior executive it's important to consider the viability of ideas and initiatives, there's just no need to present the information in such a mundane way. Of course, my ideas to challenge these structures were often met with roadblocks, except those that the team and I had control of, which we changed with abandon!

We condensed ten-page documents into one A3 page, reduced the size of templates to capture only the important information that was required, added colour and charts in place of black and white paragraphs and used images instead of bullet points in our presentations. In short, we created minimum viable documentation (MVD) and made everything we produced worth reading.

Given that white papers originated in government, the structure is generally overly formal, overly wordy and not conducive to enjoyable reading. Don't conform to this. Produce something that is challenging in its content and engaging in its presentation, rather than the other way around. The fundamental idea of a white paper is to take something that people know and understand and present a contrary perspective that gets them thinking. It can only do that if it's presented in a way that makes it easy to understand.

So, where to start?

IDEAS LIVE EVERYWHERE

Well, if you don't already have a mechanism to capture your people and customers' ideas, now would be a good time to start. Toyota is the golden child in this area and has gathered over 20 million ideas since it started collecting them in 1951; its Good Ideas Club has over 1000 members at the time of writing.

Another good example of an organisation that crowdsources ideas is AirAsia. Owner Tony Fernandes has always looked for better, smarter ways to work. He famously quit email[8] via

Twitter, then at the start of 2020 he quit Twitter and Facebook too, despite having over two million followers.[9] AirAsia's dream is 'to make flying affordable for everyone', which I'm sure you'll agree requires continual innovation. Fernandes encourages his employees to dream the impossible and considers the company a dream factory.[10]

Back in 2012, AirAsia launched its BRAIN program.[11] The acronym stood for 'Big Red Awesome Idea Network', and it provided a platform for staff to submit and vote for ideas that would improve business processes and services to achieve the organisation's dream. The best ideas inevitably bubbled to the top and were rewarded, which encouraged more ideas to be submitted. They extended the program to the public, too.

A similar exercise was undertaken at technology giant IBM. Its Innovation Jam initiative began in 2001, and from the 46,000 ideas gathered, more than ten new IBM businesses have been created, with seed funding totalling over US$10 million.[12]

Ideas don't live in a special hub where smart people hang out: they reside inside every human being, and all that's needed is a mechanism to get them out of people's heads and into the world. The white paper is one such method.

There are no hard-and-fast rules about what a white paper should look like, once you've settled on the topic that you'd like to distribute, but it should contain at least the following headings:

1. **Summary** – it's always good to start with a short abstract on the nature of the white paper. What's the problem you're seeking to address? What are the options for addressing it? What does the high-level research say? What were your conclusions? An executive summary is a great way of providing a snapshot of information so that the reader can

assess whether it's going to be of value to them to read the paper in full.

2. **Introduction** – include an outline of the problem or opportunity and the impact that it has on the business. Make this as real as you can and don't forget to talk about the human implications, too. If you focus solely on money, it will be less appealing.

3. **Value proposition** – a white paper should be packed with value, and detail the benefits that your idea will provide.

4. **Idea clarification** – this is where you break your idea down into manageable pieces of information, to allow the reader to fully understand the problem or opportunity to be addressed. You can use all manner of boxes, infographics and images to support your proposal here; just remember to keep them interesting and relevant. If it's in a 10-point font size and there are 1000 words to the page, you've fallen into the trap of writing a report that you're calling a white paper, rather than staying true to the medium.

5. **Conclusion** – wrap it up neatly and 'sell' the idea that you're proposing.

I use a design tool called Canva (canva.com) to produce my white papers, as it gives me more control over how the document looks – and also ensures that it's not in PowerPoint or Word format. That's not to say that you can't be creative with those Microsoft programs; however, most people who use them fall into the trap of being ordinary with their presentation.

There's no such thing as an ordinary idea, so never present it as such.

CULTURE HACK #18:
CHAT WITH THE CHIEF

TL;DR

- All senior managers should have an open-door policy (or no doors at all!)
- Have a monthly Q&A session with the CEO/owner.
- Have regular video updates or town hall meetings.

ONE THING TO STOP

- Boxing senior managers into offices: it creates barriers to decision-making and engagement.

I left school at seventeen with few qualifications and a burning ambition to buy more records than were currently in my collection. So, I wrote to a bank and asked for a job. They offered me an interview, then another and I was in. It really was that easy – but that was 1987 and the world was vastly different. I still have a copy of the letter I wrote, too; God knows why.

I enjoyed work almost immediately. School really hadn't been my thing: I didn't like the command-and-control nature of it and was easily distracted, and that was reflected in my results (which were rubbish). Pretty much every teacher wrote in my report card for my final year, 'Has potential but doesn't apply himself in the right way'. Fair enough.

Work was different, though. I immediately felt a connection with the people that I was working with, I enjoyed talking to the customers and there were opportunities for me to progress, if I wanted to. And I did.

In the late 1980s, the bank I was working for, NatWest, was looking to embrace technology. As a member of the 'Machine Room' (along with about ten other people my age), I sat at a big terminal that processed cheques and incoming credit slips and automatically sorted them, so we could put them in bags and send them to London. There was lots to do and we enjoyed doing it. We mixed socially, had internal sports events (see Culture Hack #25) and celebrated birthdays, anniversaries and any event we could, really.

The bank was trying to move away from its traditional ways of working. Ledger books were long gone, as were the quills used to fill them in, and there were many women in senior leadership positions, which was so refreshing in an industry that had been previously dominated by men. (Note: there is still plenty of work to do in this area, not just in banking, but everywhere.)

The bank manager, however, still had an oak-panelled office that was about the same size as our machine room, and visitors were welcomed with a warm handshake and a whisky. An affable guy in his 60s, he'd worked his way through the banking system and reached its peak. He had the big Jaguar, the personality and a fierce determination to bring in as much revenue as he could. More than that, he was a good human being who always had a smile and a joke for you, even if you were absolutely terrified of him (for no reason other than his status, it has to be said)!

Every Monday morning, without fail, he would breeze around the office and say good morning to every member of staff, often with cigar in hand. He would stop briefly to talk to certain members of staff, then move on until he'd visited every nook and cranny of the office. He only did it on a Monday and you barely saw him for the rest of the week, but it was enough for everyone to love him.

When there was something to be celebrated, he would hold court at the top of the sweeping staircase after hours and speak with confidence, pride and humour. His door was always open to the senior loans officers and he was the perfect role model of what a leader looked like to impressionable teens like myself.

About four years later, I moved onto another branch, where the manager was the antithesis of this – and it was reflected in the culture of the branch.

CULTURE STARTS AT THE TOP

Whenever I present at CEO conferences or to senior leadership teams, I make the point of reminding them that they don't own the culture of their organisation: it belongs to every single person within it. However, their behaviours, actions or inaction have the power to destroy it, almost immediately.

Research conducted by Burson-Marsteller[1] in the U.S. found that a CEO's reputation (internally and externally) accounts for 50 per cent of the organisation's reputation. In Germany, it's 63 per cent.

There have been some very high-profile stories of CEOs whose antics have adversely impacted the reputation of their organisation and their cultures. Recent examples include Travis Kalanick of Uber, Do Won Chang of Forever 21 and Adam Neumann of WeWork.

Speaking about Neumann's behaviour following the collapse of WeWork in 2019, fellow CEO and founder of Airbnb Brian Chesky said, 'I used to get advice from somebody [that said], imagine everything you do will be on the cover of *The New York Times*, because one day it very well could be'.[2]

According to researchers Hogan and Kaiser, how CEOs behave accounts for 14 per cent of the variance in organisation performance, with high performers adding an additional $25 million in value to the bottom line.[3] The old adage 'people don't leave organisations; they leave bosses' very much applies to the behaviours and actions of the person in ultimate charge.

Thirteenth-century Persian poet Jalāl ad-Dīn Muhammad Rūmī (known simply as Rumi) is believed to have been the first person to write the saying, 'A fish begins to stink at the head, not the tail',[4] which we now use in the business world as a metaphor for poor leadership. If the culture of the organisation is broken, then you have to look at who's leading it.

In my experience, the tone set by the people at the head of the organisation is the key determinant of whether the culture is vibrant or stagnant.

If CEOs and senior managers lack empathy and the ability to listen, pontificate over decisions, ignore or make excuses for poor behaviour and don't make themselves visible to those they represent, then this will very much be reflected in the culture and performance of the organisation. I don't understand why people still don't understand this.

Many people pay lip-service to culture, run engagement surveys and talk about diversity and inclusion as being the company's most important initiative. Those same people have a leadership team comprising middle-aged white men, don't action the feedback provided by staff and seemingly go out of their way to create a culture that lacks safety. Employees continue to go above and beyond to try to change things; the fortunate are able to leave for other employers, while the not-so-fortunate continue to battle mental and physical health issues brought on by the stress these environments create.

If you're a CEO or senior manager reading this, please don't be this person. You have a chance to leave a legacy of humanity and humility – why waste it?

THE IMPORTANCE OF VISIBILITY

Leadership is a choice to make a positive difference to people's lives – which means that those in positions of authority need to be visible and accessible to the people they serve.

They can't remain tucked away in their offices, shunning people and hoping that nobody talks to them. Richard Branson – someone who is always visible – said it best: 'If becoming successful meant being aloof, I never would have achieved anything'.[5] In a photo that went viral in 2016, Branson was pictured in the Virgin Australia office, smiling behind a member of staff who had fallen asleep on the sofa! Branson tweeted the picture to his eight million followers on Twitter, along with a photo of him waking the staff member up. The person in question had been on standby in between flights; however, the key takeaway for most was that Branson was actually touring the office and interacting with staff, rather than sitting in a boardroom with the senior managers.

Google measures the reputation of its managers by surveying staff on their manager's performance, as it recognises that the quality and humanity of its managers is the 'single best predictor' of whether employees stay or leave. The average score (out of 100) was 84,[6] which is a bar that most managers elsewhere would struggle to achieve.

Having the CEO and senior managers as visible and approachable as they can be is key to generating the level of engagement required to create and maintain a vibrant culture.

So, what mechanisms can you use to increase CEO visibility?

Firstly, there's the walk and greet. Not a passive dash through the office, a quick wave of the hand and a few good mornings, but a deliberate visit. The CEO must stop and talk, ask people about their weekends, what they're working on and if they have any frustrations. Nothing improves management performance more than knowing that your team could dob you in to the CEO once a week!

If the office is big, then you can choose a different department each week and get to know people's names and what they do. If the organisation is located at different sites, then travel will be necessary. Getting out and about regularly is the best way to be visible to employees.

Secondly, a monthly hour-long session could be arranged, where different members of the organisation get to have a 'chat with the chief'. This can be over a coffee, over lunch or just a chat with no food or drink involved. It can be in-person or virtual or both. There's no agenda, and a different person for each department gets nominated to attend and update the CEO or ask them questions. I introduced this at one organisation a couple of years ago and the CEO got frustrated that more people didn't want to talk to him, so he increased the number of people who could attend!

Thirdly, the CEO could introduce an 'open-door' day – a day a month when people can drop by uninvited and ask questions.

It could be a particular day of the week or a specific day in the month, but the day can't change at the last minute. Nothing says 'unapproachable' like a CEO session that's cancelled an hour before because 'something more important came up'.

Finally, the CEO could run a monthly all-staff meeting or 'town hall', as they've come to be known. The last organisation I worked for in the U.K. was a retail company, and in 2006 the managing director introduced all-staff meetings which he would run from the first floor of our former-aircraft-hangar office building. They were awesome! Town halls are a highly effective way of communicating a message once, so that everyone gets it, in an environment that can also be used to celebrate the success achieved over the last period.

One CEO who's had to become more comfortable with this idea is Daniel Ek, CEO of Spotify. As an extreme introvert, Ek preferred one-on-one communication, so he would walk and talk around the office. However, given the growth of the company, he began to find this harder to do, so he introduced town hall meetings instead. The meetings didn't replace the one-on-one interactions, they were added to them.

Like Ek, many CEOs and senior managers are uncomfortable with speaking in public. I was asked by a CEO recently how he could communicate without standing in front of a room full of people. I told him that he couldn't! People want to see and hear from the CEO; it's part of the job. Daniel Ek recognised this, too.

Speaking about this in 2018,[7] Ek said, 'A lot of leaders are way more charismatic than I am. I'm an introvert. So it was a real battle with myself... I had to change things about myself that I wasn't really comfortable changing... I got a lot of feedback on what I wasn't good enough at'. But he did it and became comfortable enough to do it again, and again.

Any of these approaches work as a mechanism to improve visibility. They'll serve to make the CEO seem more human than before, build trust, demonstrate leadership, and create the conditions for other managers to do likewise.

A Gallup survey in 2019 found that when CEOs interacted with managers on a regular basis, engagement increased by 39 per cent; and then when managers did likewise with their staff, engagement rose by 59 per cent. This is all the data you need to demonstrate the importance of being visible.[8] Engagement leads to productivity, productivity leads to results and results lead to happiness... for almost everyone involved.

CULTURE HACK #19:
GO TO THE MOVIES

TL;DR

- Arrange a trip to the movies with the team.
- Screen a movie in the office.
- Have a Netflix Party and talk about it the next day.

ONE THING TO STOP

- Talking about going to the movies, but never going.

The first movie I ever saw was a British comedy called *Carry on Camping* during the long hot English summer of 1976. It was one of 31 movies that bore the 'Carry on' name and in my opinion is second only to *Carry on at Your Convenience.*

I'm not sure it was appropriate for a seven-year-old to watch, now that I look back, but Dad liked his comedies and in the mid-1970s, if you wanted a comedy, you watched a Carry On movie. If you've never seen one of these films, you could liken them to those old bawdy seaside postcards that you used to get in England. They covered historical figures such as Cleopatra *(Carry on Cleo),* events such as the Battle of Khyber Pass *(Carry on Up the Khyber)* and there are several featuring the much-loved British health service (*Carry on Doctor, Carry on Nurse,* and so on).

The movies' stars included Sid James, Barbara Windsor, Hattie Jacques, Charles Hawtrey, Joan Sims and Kenneth Williams, to name but a few, and they were poorly paid, despite the money the movies made for the studio. What kept the actors coming back picture after picture was the camaraderie that they built between them. Like most cultures, however, there is a fine line between cult and culture, and the recurring stars often weren't as welcoming as they should have been to new actors.

Jim Dale was one such actor, and said in an interview in the (U.K.) *Daily Telegraph* in May 2020, 'I knew I was entering a clique... Kenneth Williams was probably one of my better friends although he was a real sod at times'.[1]

We saw the movie in a church hall in a place called Nefyn in North Wales. The projector was sat on top of the ice-cream fridge and halfway through they stopped the film, moved the projector and sold ice creams, while the adults had a smoke. The following year, we saw *Star Wars* at an old-fashioned picture house in Colwyn Bay (again, in North Wales, which just happened to be a two-hour drive from Liverpool back then, making it a handy – and by that I mean cheap – holiday destination).

It was one of those community theatres that had managed to survive from the golden age of movies in the 1950s. The red-velvet seats were worn and the padding non-existent, but the charm remained, especially to three young children desperate for a change of scene! The following year we saw *Grease* in the same cinema, and I was hooked.

I've loved the cinema ever since.

There's just something about the anticipation of watching a movie on a screen and filling your face with an oversized bucket of popcorn that still gets me excited to this day. Our current local cinema – a fifteen-minute walk from home – just happens to be the largest cinema screen in the world. The IMAX at Melbourne Museum took over from the Sydney IMAX as the largest when the latter was demolished in 2016.[2] Its screen is an eye-watering 32 metres wide by 23 metres tall (which is two-thirds as tall as the Arc de Triomphe[3]) and has two 4K projectors. It sold 19,000 tickets for *Star Wars Episode VII: The Force Awakens* alone in 2015 ($1.9 million worth) and had a run of 152 consecutive sold-out sessions for the release of *Avatar* in 2009.

It doesn't matter where I am in the world on my travels, I always try to visit the cinema if I can. It's a haven; a way to escape the stresses of the day and escape into another world.

LIE BACK AND RELAX

'Cinema therapy', as a term, was first used in a paper by Berg-Cross, Jennings and Baruch in 1990. They are said to have defined it as 'a form of therapy in which a therapist selects films relevant to a person in treatment's areas of concern, which the individual might view alone or with specified others'.[4] The discussion between therapist and client centres around how to be mindful when watching a movie and how to explore their reactions to it or how they related it to their own life.

The Royal College of Psychiatrists in the U.K. describes movie therapy as a 'useful aid to counselling', in which specific films are prescribed to better understand one's own emotions.[5] The techniques have been used to help children overcome the separation of their parents, as well as with adopted children with special needs. Positive results have demonstrated the value of the process in reducing impulsivity and impatience.[6]

Psychotherapist Bernie Wooder is the world leader when it comes to movie therapy, and in his 2008 book of the same name, writes that the experiences that he's had with his clients 'show the powerful therapeutic role played by movies in the healing process'.[7]

Not everyone is convinced, however, with Phillip Hodson, Fellow of the British Association for Counselling and Psychotherapy, saying, 'I can't see [movie therapy] becoming mainstream because... if you've been seriously bereaved you don't want to go to a therapist and be told to watch a film, do you?' Fair enough.

SOCIAL INTERACTION, NOT SEPARATION

However, it can be a form of therapy if you organise a group visit to the cinema. Seeing a movie is one thing, but hearing what others took from it that you didn't is something else entirely.

There's nothing like a movie to divide opinion. I really didn't like the movie *Arrival* (I *really* didn't like it) and yet my friend absolutely loved it ('Best thing I've seen in years'). We talked about it for about 20 minutes, neither one of us being able to convince the other that it was brilliant/rubbish.

It reminded me of a time about ten years earlier when my team and I went to see *Toy Story 3*. (Hey, they don't all have to be super-serious sci-fi movies.) I'm a big fan of Pixar movies and yet had been ever so slightly disappointed with *Toy Story 2*. It wasn't *The Empire Strikes Back* second film that I was expecting; in fact it was more *The Lost World: Jurassic Park,* so I was nervous to see TS3. I needn't have been, as I thought it was a brilliant way to finish the franchise. (Little did I know...)

Two of the team, however, were apoplectic with rage at its (and I'm trying to remember their words here) 'saccharine nonsense' and 'overstuffed storyline' (pun intended). It was the topic of conversation for about a week, with a couple of team members going to see it again on their own to check if they could be persuaded that it was actually pretty good. They couldn't.

Like any team activity, movie-going should be inclusive, and people should never be forced to go anywhere or do anything against their will. What I will say, however, is that when you have a vibrant culture, the team recognises the importance of social interaction, not social separation, and will willingly go along and try different things. Providing, of course, that there's a fair and equitable way of deciding what to see or do. With our movie nights, we simply picked a date in the future and then drew lots to choose who would pick the movie. That person's name was removed for the next selection, and so on.

Even if it's something you wouldn't have chosen or don't want to see, you still go along. People are often pleasantly surprised at how much they enjoy a movie, but the point is to spend time with the team and create another shared story. Our movie nights always ended with Chinese, Thai or Indian food as well, which was something else to look forward to!

Cinemas very generously provide discounts for group bookings, so we always aimed for ten people and invited people from outside our team too. The benefits that we saw from these team movie nights included:

- **Socialising** – we got the opportunity to hang out with each other in an environment that didn't require alcohol or an extrovert to keep the night going (or else spoil it for everyone).

- **Learning** – we often picked movies that increased our knowledge of a particular topic or our appreciation of others' cultures. I remember a robust climate-change conversation after watching *The Day After Tomorrow*.[8]

- **Interacting** – we would discuss the film over dinner and (if it had an impact) for about a week afterwards if any one of us felt strongly about it. The selection of the next film was also a cause of great anticipation.

- **Collaboration** – by inviting people from different areas of the organisation, we were able to build relationships much faster than we could have without the shared experience. This improved the way we worked with others.

- **Entertainment** – so much laughing. As a comedy fan, whenever it was my turn, I always picked the latest Pegg/Frost/Wright, Will Ferrell, Kristen Wiig or Bill Murray movie. Some jokes put the hooks in you or create gags that translate well in the office.

Going to the movies is just one *slice* (see what I did there?) of team culture, but it's one that people find easy to engage with. You can also screen movies and TV shows in the office. There's probably a line I need to put in here to remind you about copyright and making sure it's not a commercial showing and all of that. Follow the rules, kids. But watching *Office Space* in the office (or even episodes of *The Office*) could be a meta thing to do. You probably should leave the printers alone afterwards, though.

With the rise of Netflix, Disney+, Amazon Prime and others, we now have access to an endless amount of content, and different people get excited about different shows at different times. It's not uncommon for four people within a team to be watching eight different programs at any one time, and they end up talking past each other during procrastination breaks (see Culture Hack #3).

During the COVID-19 crisis, Netflix rolled out a new feature that integrates with the Google Chrome web browser. Called 'Netflix Party', it's an extension that allows groups of friends to watch and comment on a film or TV show. Once you've logged in, you share a viewing link with the other people you'd like to join. You then select a person to be in charge of what you'll be watching, and as you all start to watch, a chat box pops up on the right side of the screen. It can be a little fiddly getting everyone to start at the same time, but once you're there, it's really interesting. If you don't mind getting distracted by people chatting while you're watching, that is.[9]

Netflix Party was a terrific innovation at a time when everyone was self-isolating and unable to meet face-to-face in the office to talk about their favourite show.

Outside of self-isolation and social restrictions, however, going to the movies is a great way to escape the day with the rest of the team. Did you know that Zappos staff are allowed to spend six hours per quarter with each other (during what would be considered working hours) to do things such as go to the movies? They're also given $50 per month to spend on team-building. If that doesn't encourage people to socially interact rather than socially separate, then nothing will.

CULTURE HACK #20:
HOLD AN AIRBNB OFFSITE

TL;DR

- Find a space for your offsite that inspires creativity.
- Plan in time for information, action, reflection and relaxation.
- Use a skilled facilitator to ensure outcomes are achieved.

ONE THING TO STOP

- Doing the same things in a different venue and calling it an offsite.

There are so many offsite horror stories; here's one I heard while I was working in London in the early 2000s.

A small team of eight people were told by their director that they were going on a team-building day over a weekend. The director said that in advance of the day, they were going to be interviewed by two outside consultants. No mention was made of the intent or expected outcomes of the day, nor of the content of the interviews or how the information would be used.

The pre-offsite interviews lasted an hour and questions ranged from, 'How happy are you in your job?' and 'Do you understand your role?' to 'How engaged are you in what the organisation is trying to achieve?' and 'How much confidence do you have in the leadership team?' Fairly standard employee-engagement questions that referred little to the team dynamic or how people worked together.

This led to confusion and a small amount of fear, even though the director had said the event was an opportunity to get to know each other better.

A week prior to the offsite, the team members were told that they would be going to Amsterdam and that all their expenses would be covered. They weren't provided with any details about the hotel, they were just told the flight that they'd been booked onto and to make their way to the airport under their own steam.

When they got to the airport on the Friday, they were given the name of hotel that they were staying at – oh, and they discovered that the director was booked onto a different flight in business class (with his wife), while everyone else was in a cheap seat with a budget airline. The party included the two consultants, who – it turned out – were doubling as facilitators for the weekend.

The team-building day itself was by all accounts a shit-show. There was no agenda and the director didn't formally open the day by thanking everyone for giving up their weekend time, nor did he talk about what he wanted them to get out of it. He merely told them that they were in the hands of the facilitators and that 'Everyone should do as they ask'.

All of this might have been fine if the group had been experienced people who'd done this kind of thing before. However, this was a group of people in their mid-twenties who didn't really understand what they were doing there.

The facilitators then proceeded to run through the feedback that each member of staff had given, which the director questioned throughout.

This was followed by an exercise in which each member of staff had to draw a picture of an animal that they felt best represented the organisation. It was the straw that broke the camel's back. One of the participants drew a picture of a mythological creature with a head at both ends of its body (think something from *Jason and the Argonauts*), representing the fact that the person felt the two parts of the organisation were pulling in different directions. At this suggestion, the director lost control of his temper, accused staff of being disloyal to the organisation and threatened change if he didn't get what he was looking for (which he didn't actually articulate). At this point there were tears and anger from the participants, which rendered the afternoon's exercises redundant: no-one wanted to participate any further.

Left with an evening to themselves in Amsterdam, they did what you'd imagine: got drunk and took drugs. They made their way home on Sunday, and by the Monday, four of the eight people had resolved to leave the organisation.

Oh, and to top it all off, the venue that they held the session in could have been any average conference room back in London.

SPACE MATTERS

Most offsite meetings that I went on early in my career were essentially the same stuff that we normally did in meetings, but in casual clothes and a more expensive venue. There were golf clubs, sailing clubs, city-centre hotels, and the occasional boardroom in other people's offices – although never in Amsterdam.

They were all 'nice'; however, only once can I remember being impressed at an offsite venue. One was held at a football club, and not just in 'standard' meeting areas but also in changing rooms and grandstands. It inspired creativity and the outputs were better for it. True, we could have been distracted by it, but we received a short tour beforehand to sate the curiosity that may have eaten into our productive time!

The physical space in which you choose to hold your event is crucially important: almost as important as the content itself. Those who organise offsites need to provide an environment that provokes a reaction in people. That shifts their mindset to possibility. That motivates, inspires and yet at the same time allows for productive work to happen. And yes, all of this is possible! It just requires a little bit of thought and plenty of planning.

You don't have to pick the best room in the tallest building with an incredible view – spending more money on a venue doesn't mean that the quality of the outputs will be any better. A large Airbnb property might do the job just as well.

You can rent a house with ten different rooms for three days and two nights for half the cost of a hotel or conference venue, close to the city. You don't have to stay overnight, although the people organising and facilitating the session may want to arrive the day before to set the venue up, but of course, you can do sleepovers if it's not too awkward.

Note: if there's too little trust in certain individuals for you to take this approach, then you have some behavioural issues that you really need to deal with right now.

Each room can be set up as a working space, with the kitchen and outdoor areas being used to prepare food. And why not bring your own, rather than waste precious dollars on having the event catered by someone else? Everyone could commit to bringing a plate, or it could be part of the preparation.

You could have different rooms for different sections of the day, which should focus on smaller groups producing higher quality outputs. If you can avoid using whiteboards and the more 'traditional' office-based tools, then all the better for creative thinking.

You have the opportunity to change up the way you would normally do things. No-one is taking minutes, there are no parking lots (ugh), no general discussions, no PowerPoint presentations and no devices. Agree how you're going to work together at the start of the day, make sure everyone has the attitude for success, then drive for the outcomes that you're looking for. No excuses.

Deciding on what the outcomes are is really the only place to start, because if you can't articulate and have people understand this, you don't really have anything that they can get excited about. Simply saying that it's a 'strategy day' or 'leadership team offsite' isn't enough. There must be a purpose and it has to be a good one:

- Why do you need this time together?

- Does it need to be in a different environment?

- What are the challenges you face or opportunities you have that would benefit from a change of environment?

- Why now?

- Are you prepared to be completely transparent about the location, costs, attendees and agenda for the offsite? If not, why not?

- Would you agree to have it videotaped, so that staff who don't attend can see the interactions and work undertaken? If not, why not?

- What preparation is required from each individual prior to the offsite?

Organisations pay five-figure sums for these events, so there'd better be a good reason for them. That money may be better spent elsewhere, on people that may need it more.

Once the purpose is agreed, then the agenda can be set. Unless you're using the offsite to simply get to know each other better, this needs to be watertight to ensure that you get the most from your time together.

The agenda may or may not include an icebreaker, but it should definitely avoid any clichéd or old-fashioned team-building activities, particularly those that involve testing the strength of dried spaghetti.

This is where engaging the services of a skilled facilitator may be useful.

IN THE HANDS OF A PROFESSIONAL

In my experience, the facilitator sets the tone for the offsite. They make sure that everyone is prepared, the objectives are clear, the activities are productive, people are engaged throughout and that you get the outcomes you expect.

Of course, you could use an internal person for this. After all, they have working knowledge of the business and its strategy, established relationships with the attendees, historical anecdotes and stories of the culture and the challenges it's faced and, if we're being honest here, it's cheaper.

The downsides include the following:

- **Bias** – a staff member may bring existing biases (conscious and unconscious) into the way they run the event.

- **Respect** – it's a fact that internal people don't command the same level of respect as those whose job it is to run these kinds of sessions for a living.

- **Reluctance** – they may be hesitant to ask the tough questions of their peers or those 'above' them and to call out the behaviour they see.

I've witnessed all of these things; however, I've witnessed the positive, too, where an internal facilitator does a great job. If that's your plan, though, I'd always recommend bringing in someone from a different team, as that's when it works best.

So, what should you expect from an external facilitator? In the simplest terms, a great facilitator should add value to your event, even though they're not participating in the content discussions. They do this in the following ways:

- **Organisation** – they shouldn't 'fly in, fly out'; they should be actively involved in the organisation of the event. They should introduce different ideas and concepts, not be focused on creating a 'standard' approach, and should only include activities that contribute to the quality of the expected outcomes. They should ensure that all attendees are briefed and that speakers – regardless of status – rehearse so that they don't go over time or send mixed messages on the day.

- **Management** – they start by building connection within the group and ensuring that everyone understands the outcomes they are striving for. They agree on behaviour and collaboration principles, and then they should have the discipline to keep to the agenda and not allow attendees to get distracted. They need to manage behaviours, ensure that everyone's voice is heard and that information and actions are captured, and that there's a good mix of conversation, time for reflection, action and rest.

- **Entertainment** – without lighthearted moments that generate laughter, the energy will quickly dissipate. The facilitator should ensure that entertainment is well placed so as not to disrupt the flow of work, and is allowed to permeate throughout the day. Introducing 'fun' activities can actually take the fun out of them. Skilled facilitators know that, and ensure that some activities generate fun, optimism and connection rather than having to mandate the achievement of these things at the start.

- **Commitment** – at the end of the session, a facilitator will ensure that the actions that have been captured throughout are relayed back to the group, and that commitment is gained from the owners to put them into practice. They may even schedule a follow-up session three months later to ensure that everyone has done what they said they would.

An offsite meeting is a way of providing a different environment to think creatively about a challenge or an opportunity that an organisation has. When done well, it can be the most productive day of the year.

CULTURE HACK #21:
VOLUNTEER AS A GROUP

TL;DR

- Give staff time to help others.
- Have a nominated charity or group that you help.
- Doing good as a team is good for your culture as well as for others.

ONE THING TO STOP

- Allowing people to use their volunteer day as a day off or to do something they should be doing anyway (like helping at their child's school gala day!)

At the heart of some of the best cultures that I've been fortunate to be part of was generosity without recognition. That is, people giving up their time, knowledge and (sometimes) money without wanting anything in return. This is a rare gift in our sometimes-selfish world. Often, it feels like people do something good, but then gleefully tell you about it or plaster it all over their social-media feed in the hope of recognition (#humblebrag).

I thought a lot about this sentence after I wrote it, as I don't want to appear cynical or disapproving of good deeds. I just feel that if you want praise for your generosity, then it's not really that generous at all. Do you know what I mean? It's like Superman hanging around for thanks every time he saved Lois Lane. Which happened 31 times in the DC Animated Universe, in case you're interested.[1] Oh, and to balance that out, Lois saved Superman 15 times.[2]

It's definitely a much more generous world today than the one I grew up in. That's not to say that there weren't great acts of generosity back then; it just wasn't as easy to do. You could set up a direct debit to pay a particular amount of money each month to a charity (my mum did this to the National Children's Home), or you could donate to a collection fund at church or in the street.

The news at the time reported facts without empathy or emotion and we saw tragedies as news events, rather than opportunities to do our bit to help people. And then one BBC news report changed everything.

On 23 October 1984, a news report from Michael Buerk in northern Ethiopia was beamed into homes around the U.K. on the six o'clock news. No-one had seen pictures quite like those broadcast during the report that evening, which talked of a drought and 'biblical famine'. Buerk walked slowly through villages while the camera showed the human catastrophe that was unfolding. In one picture, he held an emaciated child, which had my mum and millions of others in tears. Buerk called that area of Ethiopia 'the closest thing to hell on earth'.[3]

Watching that night was Robert Frederick Zenon ('just call me Bob') Geldof,[4] lead singer of the band The Boomtown Rats, along with his then-wife Paula Yates. Devastated by what he'd seen, Geldof resolved to do something to help. At the time Yates was co-presenter of the music TV show *The Tube* and one of their guests the following week were Ultravox, whose lead singer Midge Ure was similarly affected by what he'd seen.[5]

While Yates was chatting to Ure post-show, Geldof asked to speak to him and they agreed that they would work together to write a song, the proceeds of which would go to help the people starving. A week later, Ure had written the music, to which Geldof added lyrics (which he'd previously written for a Boomtown Rats song). While Ure wrote the music, Geldof had been on the phone persuading the great and good of British pop music at the time to be involved.

On 25 November 1984, at SARM studios in Notting Hill, London, between the hours of 11 a.m. and 7 p.m., artists such as U2, Boy George, Phil Collins, Duran Duran, Bananarama, Spandau Ballet, Wham, Status Quo, Paul Weller and Paul Young got together to record the song, 'Do they know it's Christmas?'[6]

The single sold over two million copies around the world and raised almost £28 million (US$24 million). Almost every family in our neighbourhood had a copy of the £1.35 single, there were Ethiopian charity events and all church events donated a portion of their takings to the Ethiopian fund. Everyone wanted to do their bit.

Live Aid followed in July 1985, raising over £150 million after staging events in London and Philadelphia. Halfway through the event, frustrated that people weren't being generous enough, Geldof famously lost his temper live on air and started effing and jeffing to shake people into action. It worked. After the outburst, donations to the cause increased to £300 per second!

A CULTURE OF GIVING

There's a popular, yet incorrect narrative touring the globe that the latest generation (as other, older generations like to call them) are self-centred. Of course, every generation of people has always blamed the one before it and despaired of the one after it, so this is true to form. Except that the assertion of Gen Z (people born from 1997 onwards) being self-centred is wholly inaccurate. They care deeply about the world and the plight of humans within it and will readily give their time or money to help.

Indeed, in a Glassdoor survey in 2018, 60 per cent of Gen Z members interviewed said that they wanted to have a positive impact on the world, compared to 39 per cent of Millennials.[7] Both generations, however, expect much more from the organisations they work for, with purpose being as important as pay cheque in their decisions around where they want to work.

It's not just the under-40s who are putting this pressure on, either. Post-global financial crisis the emphasis on organisations to do good – rather than be greedy – has increased around the world, leading to 181 U.S. CEOs agreeing to take a different approach to their predecessors.

CEOs from organisations such as Amazon, Cisco, JPMorgan Chase, Walmart and Apple agreed on a new *Statement on the Purpose of a Corporation* that centred around 'People – Planet – Profit', in that order. This is their investment in what we call corporate social responsibility (CSR). There are four commitments that underpin the purpose statement:

1. Taking care of our employees

2. Investing in our people

3. Building communities, meeting challenges

4. Preparing tomorrow's innovators

Time will tell whether they deliver on these; however, that's not going to stop individuals and other organisations from creating their own culture of giving.

Volunteering is described as 'time willingly given for the common good and without financial gain'; in fact, it might even cost you something. Most organisations now offer volunteer time off (VTO) to their staff, providing payment in exchange for their people doing good in the world. In order to help people find activities that require volunteers, online classified company Seek has set up a specific website at volunteer.com.au.

The Society for HR management's 2018 Employee Benefits Report shows that nearly 1 in 4 companies in the U.S. are using VTOs for competitive advantage.[8] That is to say, they're demonstrating that they're doing their bit to pay it forward and hoping that people take notice.

Not everyone organisation provides its staff with VTOs, however, with only half of those surveyed by Salesforce providing paid time to volunteer.[9]

The benefits gained by organisations who provide staff with time to volunteer include:

- **Reputation** – not only is it good for the organisation's external reputation, but staff pride also increases and they are proud to tell others about what they are doing.

- **Connection** – when teams work together on volunteer projects, it increases the connection between them and aids future collaboration.

- **Empathy** – not only for each other in the volunteer work that's undertaken, but also for the people who they're helping.

- **Capability** – there's a good chance that by working on projects that fall outside their work roles and responsibilities, people will pick up new skills that will benefit them inside and outside the office.

- **Loyalty** – organisations that consistently allow their staff to give back and also find ways to do so as an organisation will attract loyalty from staff and customers alike.

In a 2016 article, Peter Baines, author of *In Doing Good by Doing Good*, recommends that organisations answer five questions if they're looking at making volunteering part of their CSR plan:[10]

1. Is there a strategy behind your volunteering?

2. Is it aligned to your values?

3. Who is it really designed to benefit, and are those who are meant to benefit from the program, in fact doing so?

4. Can we re-engineer our volunteering to create a multiplier effect or shared experience?

5. What is the return to our business and how are we measuring it?

WORKING TOGETHER FOR THE GREATER GOOD

For this culture hack, I want to focus on question number four, particularly around creating a shared experience.

Here in Australia, the average person gives up 2.5 hours per week to volunteer, with these hours increasing over the last 10 years. Clean Up Australia is the greatest beneficiary of those hours, with over three-quarters of a million volunteers – which is ten times the next highest, Surf Life Saving New South Wales.[11] These numbers have increased over the last decade.

As I mentioned earlier, by working together on these projects you can increase the connection between members of the culture or create connections by inviting others to join in the activity.

Here are some ideas for group volunteering:

- Assemble care packages.

- Clean up a public space.

- Hold unique workplace fundraisers.

- Donate blood.

- Plant and grow a community garden.

- Build wheelchairs.

- Build bicycles for children.

- Go grocery shopping on behalf of those unable to do it themselves.

- Do a 10,000 step challenge.

- Participate in a fun run.

You could incorporate a competitive element to your volunteering – around funds raised or hours given – in order to further serve the community. Or else you could create a theme.

One organisation in the U.S. organises what it calls the 'End-Hunger Games' for teams to participate in. Challenges are set that enable teams to 'earn' non-perishable food items as prizes. The aim is for each team to win as many challenges as possible and therefore collect as many food items as they can. At the end, they then have to work together to build the most impressive structure from their items.

The judges look for creativity, style and form and award a prize to the best structure, which (I'd like to think) isn't always necessarily the biggest. All food collected is then donated to each team's nominated food bank.[12]

Over the years, I've volunteered in a soup kitchen, repaired sand dunes, collected donations on the street, built furniture and many other things with my teammates. Each volunteering exercise not only resulted in us helping those less fortunate than ourselves, but also brought us closer together. The shared stories that we were able to add to our vibrant culture were the unexpected benefits of our time in service to others, and we looked forward to those volunteer events every year.

Giving up your time to help others who don't have what you have will always be the most productive use of your time.

CULTURE HACK #22:
LEAVE THE LAPTOP AT WORK

TL;DR

- Presenteeism is a bad thing.
- Make flexible working something that aids productivity, not burnout.
- Don't take your laptop home with you.

ONE THING TO STOP

- Doing anything other than taking notes on your laptop in a meeting.

In December 2019, Shopify CEO Tobi Lütke shocked the business world and put thousands of senior managers to shame with one sentence: 'I'm home at 5.30 p.m. every evening'.[1] There was a collective 'WHAAAAAAAAAA?' at the idea that the CEO of a billion-dollar software company had time for both work and family.

The narrative from many senior people around the world is quite the opposite, with the number of hours 'worked' being worn as a badge of honour. Eighty hours a week is portrayed as commitment, productivity or loyalty, when in reality it often suggests poor prioritisation or an inability to focus on the job at hand.

It's not like that 80 hours is all productive work, either. One study from the Boston University Questrom School of Business found that managers could not distinguish between those who had done a 'real' 80 hours a week and those who faked it.

If expectations are set correctly at the start of the week, you know exactly how productive someone has been and also whether they need to do more hours to ensure they hit their targets. Adding an extra hour or two to get a task completed is different to the presenteeism bug that most organisations seem to have caught.

Presenteeism – that is, the practice of working longer than is necessary – is now just as much of a problem as absenteeism. It's unhealthy and can have lasting effects on individuals and the cultures that they work in. Presenteeism leads to burnout, which, according to a survey from Kronos people leaders, affects 95 per cent of its workforce.[2]

German-born American psychologist Herbert J. Freudenberger is credited with inventing the term 'burnout' in 1974, when in a paper he referred to it as a 'loss of motivation, growing sense of emotional depletion, and cynicism' that he'd observed when working at a clinic in New York.[3]

Burnout is not a medical condition per se: it's a term that's used to describe periods of extreme work-related stress. This stress leads to exhaustion that impairs both mental and physical performance, which often leads to alienation, procrastination or, worse, illness.

THE TWELVE STAGES OF BURNOUT

Freudenberger, along with fellow psychologist Gail North, described twelve stages of burnout, which are:

1. **A compulsion to prove oneself** – excessively attempting to prove your worth to others.

2. **Working harder** – taking on more to demonstrate your uniqueness.

3. **Neglecting needs** – no time for self-care, family or friends.

4. **Displacement of conflicts** – dismissal of problems, often leading to panic. Physical symptoms emerge.

5. **Revision of values** – values are focused purely on work.

6. **Denial of emerging problems** – intolerance of others, cynicism, aggression, increased difficulty with building relationships.

7. **Withdrawal** – social life is non-existent; you may turn to alcohol or drugs to relieve stress.

8. **Behavioural changes** – family and friends notice a difference and become concerned.

9. **Depersonalisation** – seeing neither yourself nor others as valuable; becoming unaware of your own needs.

10. **Inner emptiness** – feeling empty and attempting to 'fill' this by over overeating, drinking or taking drugs.

11. **Depression** – feeling lost and unsure; being unable to see any kind of positive future.

12. **Burnout syndrome** – which can include total mental and physical collapse, and requires medical attention.[4]

I've been at level 9 and 10 many times in my career (including very recently) and 11 and 12 once or twice, at which point I needed help.

Christina Maslach, Professor Emerita of Psychology at the University of California, Berkeley, has been studying burnout since the late 1970s and has written many books and papers on the subject.

In an interview in 2019, she said that toxic workplace culture is to blame for burnout:

> *There's more destructive competition. I cannot tell you how many people talk about socially toxic workplaces, where you don't trust anybody because they're going to try and throw you under the bus and get rid of you as competition.*[5]

According to one report into presenteeism and burnout, the hidden costs are equivalent to a 2.6 per cent loss in productivity and a 2.7 per cent loss in gross domestic product.[6] Then there are the people who take annual leave but end up working through it, or taking their work home with them. This is the lesser-known (yet often equally troublesome) problem of 'leaveism'.

Almost three-quarters of respondents to a Chartered Institute of Personnel and Development (CIPD) survey in the U.K. said that they'd observed leaveism over the past twelve months.[7]

Almost every person will feel some level of burnout throughout the year if they don't take steps to address their habits, practices and lifestyle, especially in a work environment. Organisations need to realise this and ensure that their cultures are psychologically safe and don't consider the number of hours that someone is in the office to be a measure of success. They also need to ensure that people are taking the required amount of annual leave and aren't working during it, to get the rest they need to recover.

Despite the thousands of words devoted to presenteeism and the fact that most organisations have mental-health guidelines, the aforementioned CIPD survey found that less than a third of them were taking action to address it.

By contrast, Tobi Lütke said of the Shopify culture, 'We don't burn out people. We give people space. We love real teams with real friendship forming'.[8] This is where a culture needs to be.

BE FLEXIBLY DISCIPLINED

One of the positive things to come out of the COVID-19 crisis was an increase in empathy. As everyone was suddenly working from home, managers took an interest in how people were coping and the situations that they faced at home. Many employees were actively encouraged to take breaks from screens and ensure they got the right amount of rest.

Of course, post-COVID-19, coming into the office while sick is a definite no-no; however, as people become more comfortable working from home, the temptation to get the laptop out or turn the PC on, instead of recovering, is ever-present. So, there's still some work to do.

I'm a big supporter of flexible working, but only if it supports healthy balance for employees and doesn't increase the stress on them or their lives.

As a result of COVID-19, barriers to more people working flexibly were finally removed – it's just a shame that it took a global pandemic for managers to act. Thanks to an investment in collaboration tools and a commitment to working differently, it's never been easier for employees to work remotely. Faster internet connections and the evolution of technology will provide further opportunities for organisations to reduce their office space and save time and money as a result.

Cisco is one organisation that's on to this. Almost 90 per cent of its employees telecommute once a week. It saves over three million hours of commuting, providing the organisation with $270 million more productive time and stopping over 47,000 tons of carbon from being pumped into the atmosphere. The numbers for remote working certainly stack up.[9]

Having a well-defined culture provides the foundation for great remote working. Agreement on the six pillars of culture (as I wrote about in my book *Culture Fix*) – personality and communication, vision, values, behaviour, collaboration and innovation – ensures that everyone understands what's expected of them at all times, and keeps them both physically and emotionally connected.

If your organisation has yet to do this work, then here are six tips – three for the organisation, three for the individual – for more effective and productive flexible working.

For the organisation

1. Trust your people

It seems ridiculous to start with this point, but I still think that many organisations see trust as something that needs to be 'earned' rather than 'assumed'. One survey found that 78 per cent of people don't fully trust their workmates! If you've taken the time and effort to hire people who have the technical and emotional skills to do the job, then set expectations clearly and let them get on with it. If you expect the worst of people, then it's likely that you'll get it.[10]

2. Invest in collaboration tools

There are literally hundreds of tools that you can use to stay connected, and you should be using one regardless of whether people are working remotely or not, in order to cut down on the amount of emails sent (see Culture Hack #1). It's important that you pick one and then ensure that everyone is trained in how to use it properly, that it's used consistently and that it evolves over time to stay relevant and support productive work.

3. Set expectations well

By far the biggest issue with flexible working is the fact that expectations are neither set nor managed well. This includes expectations around how the individual sets themselves up for success (see the next section), about when they should be online and offline or simply about the quality of their deliverables. When expectations are set and managed well, the work gets done.

For the individual

1. Set up your workspace

Just because you're not in the office doesn't mean that you shouldn't set up your workspace properly. To work from home effectively, you need a good internet connection, a laptop (PC or Mac) with all of the right applications installed and preferably a light-filled space in which to work. You also need to remove all distractions to allow you to focus on the job at hand.

2. Establish your routines

No lounging around in your PJs all day, let's deal with that one first. While you don't have to get dressed in office attire, you still *have* to get dressed, unless your surname is Lebowski! Your attitude must be right and you can't be putting the washing on or popping to the shops when there's work to be done. The simple rule when working from home is to ask yourself, 'Would I do this if I were in the office?' If the answer is no, then it can wait until you finish for the day, whatever time that is.

3. Stay in constant contact

Working flexibly can be a lonely business, so it's critically important that you stay in touch. Chat tools can help, but it's also nice to see another face or speak to someone on the phone. Videoconferencing is so simple to use these days that it's a mistake not to use it. Oh, and when people dial you in for meetings, you have to remain focused – you can't be tapping away on your laptop or nipping to get a drink. Don't forget the simple rule from point number 2!

∞

Individuals need to be disciplined about when they 'close down' for the day, whether they're working in the office or working remotely. The focus needs to be on the outcomes expected, rather than setting yourself a long list of 'stuff to get done'.

Having the discipline to put the laptop away or leaving it in the office will help to ensure that you never get past burnout stage 1, which is crucial for your productivity and mental health.

Ask yourself these questions:

- Have I completed everything I set out to achieve today?

- Am I on track to achieve this week's outcomes?

- Have I prepared an achievable list of tasks to undertake tomorrow?

If the answer is yes to all of these questions, then the PC or Mac can be shut down. If you're using a laptop, are in the office and have answered yes to all of these questions, then find somewhere safe where it can be stored and leave it there to collect in the morning. You'll likely create a list of excuses as to why you need to lug it home with you, but they are simply that: excuses.

It's time to turn off, tune out and reconnect with what's important.

CULTURE HACK #23:
JOB SWAP

TL;DR

- Find development opportunities for people based on their interests.
- Create a job-rotation program.
- Tailor development to the needs of the individual.

ONE THING TO STOP

- Putting everyone on the same professional development program and hoping for culture change.

Greensboro, North Carolina is the 68th most populous city in the U.S., with 270,000 people, and sits midway between Washington and Atlanta. It's home to the International Civil Rights Center & Museum, the Wet 'n Wild Emerald Pointe water park and the Greensboro Science Center.[1]

It's also home to the Center for Creative Leadership (CCL), a global education provider.[2]

If you live outside the U.S., you may not have heard of Greensboro or even the CCL. You definitely won't have heard of researchers Morgan McCall, Michael M. Lombardo and Robert A. Eichinger, who worked there; and yet, if you're in an HR role or have ever requested any training from the Center, then you'll almost certainly have heard of their most notable work. In the mid-1980s, they produced a paper that summarised their investigation into the key developmental experiences of successful people managers.

They found that the most beneficial way for people to learn or refine new work-related skills, interact with influential people within a business, address challenges and opportunities and make decisions was via hands-on experience. They recommended that this form 70 per cent of people's development time.

The next best way to develop these skills was through interacting with others in the organisation – coaching, mentoring and social interaction, which includes things such as communities of practice, subject-matter networks and collaboration platforms. An important facet of this is receiving constructive feedback and encouragement. They recommended that this form 20 per cent of people's development time.

The final element of development is the provision of a formal training program or education event from practitioners with academic backgrounds. They recommend that this form 10 per cent of people's development time.[3]

This approach became known as the '70-20-10 rule' and became the standard answer from HR whenever you asked to go on a training course that they either didn't want to fund or didn't have the money to fund.

Of course, this approach assumes, as the education system does, that everyone learns in exactly the same way – which they don't. I have a friend who needs to understand all of the theory of a job first, after which he likes to talk to people who already do it, before being pitched into the deep end himself. For him the equation is the other way around – 70 per cent education, 20 per cent interaction, 10 per cent on the job.

Based on my own experiences, however, I believe that it's only when you do a job and interact with people and issues in real time that you gain that full understanding of how to do it well. So the original equation works well for me.

Most workplace cultures focus the 70-20-10 on the person's current role, which is certainly a way to mastery. In his book *Atomic Habits,* James Clear describes mastery as habits plus deliberate practice. At some stage in every employee's tenure, they will have developed the habits and had enough deliberate practice, to have mastered what they have to do. At this point there are two options: mastery in another area or the road to eventual boredom.

STICK OR TWIST?

For some, the road to boredom is attractive, because it's easier, less stressful and (in some cases) offers a path to retirement. For people who want more from their professional life, however, it's a dead end that they can see no way out of.

According to a Korn Ferry survey of 5000 professionals in 2008, the number-one reason that people look for a new job is that they're bored in their current job.[4] Boredom eventually leads to disengagement: the employee loses the connection to their team, becomes disillusioned with what the organisation is trying to achieve and 'checks out' of the activity required to keep the culture vibrant.

When this disengagement becomes widespread, it hits the organisation hard. Productivity dips, targets are missed, deadlines slip, good people leave, and the costs can be enormous.

According to the last State of the American Workforce report produced by Gallup, only a third of the U.S. workforce are engaged in their role. The cost of this disengagement to the American economy is between $483 billion and $605 billion in lost productivity every year.[5]

Generationally, people are spending less and less time in each job, which means that unless action is taken, this becomes a perpetual problem. It's estimated that Millennials in the tech sector alone switch jobs on average every 1.8 years; to address this and build loyalty, organisations need to think creatively about how they can retain people.

One idea is to provide people with the opportunity to try different roles, either within their own department or in the wider organisation.

Traditionally, these opportunities have been handled as secondments. With a secondment, a temporary vacancy arises in another department and internal applicants can apply to fill that role for the time that it's estimated to be vacant. These are great short-term opportunities to provide exposure to a role or skill set in another area, and may help employees to determine where their future lies, or else provide skills cover for the organisation.

Secondments, however, usually require someone else to be absent for a particular period, or rely on a role being established that the organisation wishes to resource temporarily.

A much better idea – in my experience – is to make job rotation part of the employee experience. It should be something that's expected, anticipated and welcomed as a way of evolving one's skill set and staving off the inevitable boredom of a single role.

This approach is already practised in some of the great workplace cultures. Spotify doesn't keep people in the same job for longer than two years. You undertake a 'mission' for no longer than 24 months, then you move onto another role. CEO Daniel Ek explains, 'You may have the same title, but you don't have the same job more than two years, and the more honest we are about that, the better it is'.[6]

LinkedIn has a similar approach, but calls the rotations 'Tours of Duty'.

This is something that I did with my team; however, I looked to rotate my management team into each other's roles for a month at a time. On a couple of occasions, this led to permanent job swaps as people found their niche.

The benefits to the individual are as follows:

- **It staves off boredom** – there's reduced opportunity to become stale in a role.

- **They learn a new skill set** – which opens people up to new skills, methods and techniques.

- **They uncover hidden talents** – the rotation may unlock potential that wasn't previously known.

The benefits to the team and organisation as are follows:

- **Reduced chance of culture stagnating** – it leads to continual cultural evolution and refreshment.

- **Increased resilience** – by cycling through different roles, people are better able to deal with issues that come their way.

- **Improved empathy between team members** – when everyone understands each other's role and its demands, it increases the connection between them.

- **Improved communication** – because of improved empathy, employees are better able to communicate with each other in a language everyone understands.

- **Improved performance** – different people get the opportunity to set different performance levels.

- **Greater innovation** – different eyes and ears bring creative thinking to established issues or opportunities for improvement.

- **Reduced turnover** – keeping people's skill sets fresh and investing in their development means they are more likely to stay with the organisation.

- **Reduction in single points of failure** – by creating an army of people with generalist skills, you reduce the likelihood of losing the skills previously held by one individual.

- **Better succession planning** – by providing opportunities to try different roles, you increase the number of people that you're able to place in roles.

Of course, there are some downsides, too, although these pale in comparison to the benefits. They are:

- **Loss of specialised staff** – there are people who simply want to do the one thing they were hired to do, and they may leave if they feel they're being forced into a position they don't want.

- **Reduced continuity** – hand-offs take time, which may mean there is a loss of continuity.

- **Reduced productivity** – with different people cycling through different roles, it might take cultures a bit of time to adapt.

There may be others; however, in the times that I rotated people through different roles I never lost any of my specialised staff and any productivity dips were always short-lived.

A PATHWAY TO THE FUTURE

Implementing a structured job-rotation program allowed me to address the 70 per cent development as outlined by McCall, Lombardo and Eichinger. My people strategy centred around providing opportunities for people to develop and stretch themselves and to experience roles that they'd never really thought about doing.

Of course, this approach doesn't work for everyone, in every team, in every organisation. I never rotated people if we had high-impact issues that had to be managed (although some shadowing provided an opportunity to learn) or to avoid dealing with performance issues, which is often what others do. The development plan was deliberate and enabled me to create a succession plan and pathway that was visible and provided staff with optimism that their future lay with the organisation.

To implement a similar experience, you need to think about the following things:

- **Culture definition** – teams need to have defined their culture to make it easier to integrate new members and ensure that vibrancy is maintained regardless of personality or skill set. (This is true whether you have job rotation or not!)

- **Competency and interest mapping** – create a database of people's skills and interests so that you can look for opportunities relevant to them.

- **Role playbooks** – establish playbooks for each role, so that rotation becomes easier. Without the playbook you rely on verbal handovers, which can often be lengthy or else not comprehensive enough to provide the context for the person coming into the role.

- **Coaching and mentoring** – inevitably with job rotation, not all the information can be provided in a playbook. Therefore, it's important that people have the skills to be able to coach and mentor others, or else you need to provide an external person to support the process.

- **Being great at feedback** – you must ensure that feedback is given regularly and focuses on behaviours, not skills.

- **Setting goals** – ensure that it's not just a case of keeping a different seat warm, but that each person has a set of goals (beyond learning new skills) by which their performance can be evaluated. After all, there's still a business to run!

- **Communication** – everyone needs to understand the approach that you're taking and why you're taking it. Preferably, you need to have your People and Culture team help you design it. On one occasion they let me do it myself, but I always felt better having their support and input.

- **Setting expectations early** – when hiring new people, you must ensure that they're aware of the opportunities for job rotations, so they know what to expect when they start.

The job-rotation program was supplemented with the 20 per cent on social interaction and 10 per cent on formal professional development; for the most part, however, the teams got what they were looking for from their exposure to other roles and other departments.

Providing the merry-go-round doesn't move too quickly, rotating people through different roles is a great way to keep individuals and the culture fresh and ensure that boredom and stagnation don't creep in.

CULTURE HACK #24:
RECORD A CULTURE VIDEO

TL;DR

- Video is a great way to showcase your purpose, values and culture.

- Don't overthink it, be authentic and use your own people.

- Think about ways you can serve your customers or staff through video content.

ONE THING TO STOP

- Thinking that video is the future. It was... about ten years ago. You need to get onto it, today.

The odds of you dying in a plane crash are anywhere between 1 in 5 million to 1 in 20 million, depending on which survey you read. However, one thing is certain: they're pretty slim. You're four times more likely to be hit by lightning (but it's still a slim chance at 1 in 1.2 million), and yet flying is one of the biggest fears that people have. As many as 25 per cent of passengers[1] have some form of fear when they get onto a plane, and since the authorities don't want people panicking when they're 30,000 feet up, they try to manage that risk before taking off.[2]

Prior to the introduction of screens, this risk was managed by flight attendants, who read from a pre-prepared card a list of the things that you needed to be aware of in case of any issues during the flight. It told you the things you could do and couldn't do, although interestingly, at one point you couldn't use a pager on a plane but could still smoke!

In the mid-1980s, TV screens started to appear and the role of the flight attendants in the safety procedure was diminished to demonstrating life jackets, pointing to exits and directing your eyes to the escape lighting. A former flight attendant friend of mine is still grateful for the screen introduction, saying, 'Strapping a dusty mask that's been used by hundreds of different people over my face was the least enjoyable part of my job'.

At first these videos were merely instructional. 'Do this. Don't do that. If this happens, don't do this, but then definitely do that. Oh, but not like that: like this instead. And when that's done, then do this. Unless you have a child, then do this first, then do that, unless this should happen in which case do the other.'

You know what I mean.

Around the mid-1990s, things started to change.[3] It was still crucially important to mitigate the flying fear risk – because the brace position still isn't going to save you if your plane actually crashes – however, airlines found that they could mitigate further by introducing things like entertainment and, even better, laughter!

Virgin Atlantic was one of the first to take it to the next level in the late 1990s[4] with animations. Sister airline Virgin America doubled down in 2007 with their campaign to 'Make Flying Fun Again!' At a time when viral videos were just becoming a thing, Virgin America dominated.[5]

Most of the flying that I'd done prior to 2007 was to Europe and the U.S. from the U.K., so every video was a bit, well, boring. But in September 2007 we moved to New Zealand, and after taking my first flight with Air New Zealand the following year, my video expectations were forever reset.

If you haven't seen an Air New Zealand safety video, then you should head to YouTube immediately and search for them. There are too many great ones to mention them all, so I'll tell you about my favourite.

Called 'The Most Epic Safety Video Ever Made', it was released in 2014 to coincide with the launch of *The Hobbit: The Battle of the Five Armies* and directed by the fantastic Taika Waititi.[6] Waititi also stars in the video alongside Elijah Wood, Sylvester McCoy and Peter Jackson himself. However, it's not all movie stars, as Air New Zealand also used its own flight crew in the videos. To date, the video has almost 20 million views on YouTube, most by people who will never be fortunate enough to fly with Air New Zealand, but who now have an aspiration to do so, based on what they've seen.

PUTTING YOUR CULTURE OUT THERE

That's the real genius of the safety videos – they provide the organisation with the opportunity to put the purpose, values and culture of the company out into the public domain for all to see. And of course, it doesn't have to be a safety video: it can be any video, because video is where it's at right now.

According to one Cisco report,[7] by 2022, video will account for 82 per cent of internet traffic, and almost half of all devices in the world will be video-capable. Much of that has to do with an idea that former PayPal employees Jawed Karim, Steve Chen and Chad Hurley had in 2005.

Following the Janet Jackson costume furore during Super Bowl XXXVIII in 2004, the three realised that there wasn't one location online where people could watch videos. Twelve months later, in December 2005, YouTube was born. Their first video was of Karim talking about the length of an elephant's trunk at the zoo, which of course, can still be viewed on, er, YouTube! It's called 'Me at the Zoo' if you want to check it out.[8]

A year later, Google realised the huge potential of the platform and paid (what seems to be now the ridiculously small sum of) $1.65 billion for it.[9] YouTube is now second only to Google.com as the most popular website in the world.

Speaking of Google, it went one step further than the airlines and permitted an entire movie to be shot of its culture – well, at least, how I imagine its culture could be. *The Internship* is a 2013 comedy that stars Vince Vaughn and Owen Wilson as former salespeople who get fired, but then manage to get internships at Google. I won't spoil it for you because you should watch it, if only to see how it showcases the Google campus and elements of its culture – from the free bikes to get from one campus to the next to the funky office space (although the Georgia Tech campus was also used for the film). The Google owners agreed to co-operate, providing that the director, Shawn Levy, didn't make the movie mean-spirited.

Of course, the internship program shown in the film isn't a replica of Google's; however, it was still free advertising from a movie that took almost $100 million at the box office. Facebook, by comparison, refused to participate in *The Social Network* movie, and I'm not sure I'd have enjoyed the film as much if it had![10]

Many organisations have taken the leap and recorded videos showcasing their culture that can be easily found online. There are some great examples from Zendesk; Dropbox, which uses

Muppets (as in puppets, not rubbish staff members!); Southwest Airlines, which has videos of what it's like to be a pilot; and one of my favourites, Vistaprint.

Vistaprint has a 'Life in Vistaprint' section on its site where staff talk about the organisation's policies on things like flexible working, team outings and how they help and support their customers. The company has a motto – 'Very small, big company' – which runs through its videos, and everything links back to its values of passion, perseverance and possibilities.

Vistaprint also produces online programs, simple 'how-to' guides and staff interviews and has lots of fun things you can do with its products. The company has embraced video to engage not only its customers, but potential staff, too. And with over 6000 employees in twelve countries, it's always on the lookout for talent.

WHY BOTHER?

Incredibly, despite the statistics around the use of video, there are some organisations that haven't yet embraced its power. So, for those people, I thought I would articulate some reasons why they should, to help them overcome their 'Why bother?' or 'We have more important things to do' mindset.

Video shows humanity

Principally, the reason you should invest in video is that it makes the organisation appear human. It removes barriers to people's knowledge of you and offers an opportunity to welcome customers and employees alike, while providing a simple way of delivering a message.

You can tell your story

Video is a way for the organisation to creatively share its origin story, which is always best done through staff stories. Where did it start? What challenges has it overcome? Who were the key people involved and how does their legacy live on? When done well, these stories elicit feelings and encourage people to find out more about what the organisation does.

It sells your culture

Video provides an opportunity for organisations to clearly demonstrate how they live out their values, show the work that they're doing in pursuit of their vision and show how their people behave and collaborate with each other. Videos can also be used to talk about the organisation's purpose, which almost two-thirds of Millennials are as interested in as they are the wage they'll be paid.

By putting the culture into the public domain, you're seeking to attract people who share the organisation's ideals and viewpoints, and build up a talent pool should you need to recruit.

It sells the benefits

Whether it's health care, child care, further education or opportunities for advancement, when people explain how they've been helped or supported, it's much more powerful to show the difference benefits make than have half a dozen dot-points on a webpage.

It demonstrates uniqueness

All of this contributes to the uniqueness of the organisation. Video provides a chance to show the 'special sauce' of the organisation. More than where it came from, what it stands for, the environment in which people work or the benefits provided to staff, people want to picture how they'll be happy in *this* organisation compared to others.

What better way to do this than to show a 'day-in-the-life' of your staff to allow people to see just that? You might even want to engage a virtual-reality company to help you to physically do this! Just let that quirky, unique way you do things shine through.

It goes without saying that any organisation that attempts to put forward an image of itself that's different from reality will get found out very quickly indeed. Social media seems to have been designed to highlight things such as this, and many organisations have fallen foul of it. Your videos need to be authentic, real and based on things that really do happen! If you don't have a green space to picnic and play Quidditch on, but there's one in your video, then you can expect to find yourself on the front page of *The Quibbler* in no time.

CULTURE HACK #25:
HOLD AN INTERDEPARTMENTAL SPORTS DAY

TL;DR

- Having a winning mentality is important to team success.
- Create a mixed-gender sports team to add fun and competitiveness.
- Get teams together to compete against each other.

ONE THING TO STOP

- Thinking that winning is a bad thing, but remember that winning at all costs most definitely is.

Vincent Thomas Lombardi was born in Brooklyn, New York, on 11 June 1913. He played sports at the Catholic high school that he attended, but had poor eyesight and wasn't the most athletic person on the team. Nonetheless, he persevered.

Deciding to pursue American football instead of a career in the priesthood, he received a scholarship to Fordham University in the Bronx. He was a committed and talented player, but just not big enough or strong enough to play professionally. He drifted from job to job – this was during the Great Depression – but then in 1939 his life changed.

Aged 26, Lombardi wanted to marry his then-girlfriend and start a family, so he needed a steady job. An old teammate of his at Fordham University offered him a job as an assistant football coach at St Cecilia High School in New Jersey – he would never look back.

Three years later, Lombardi took over as head coach and the St Cecilia team was recognised as the best high school team in the nation. This led to him returning to his previous college and becoming coach of the Fordham freshman football team in 1947. But it would be his next job that had the biggest impact on his coaching style: he took up the role of assistant coach at the U.S. Military Academy at West Point, New York. Prior to his time at West Point, Lombardi had a spiritual style of coaching and created strong bonds with his players.

The academy, however, provided him with a level of discipline he hadn't seen before, and he added this to his spiritual style of coaching. He recognised that the attributes of a winning team combine behaviours such as drive, motivation, courage and discipline with collaboration, humility, positivity and empathy. Lombardi was able to demonstrate those behaviours in spades and to coach his players on them, not only on the skills that were required for success.

He got his break in the National Football League (NFL) in 1954, as a coach with the New York Giants. However, it was his time as head coach of the Green Bay Packers from 1960 to 1967 that would cement his reputation as one of the greatest coaches of all time.

His Green Bay team won its division three out of five years and won the NFL championship twice in this time. It finished second in its division in 1963 and 1964, but then won it all (including Super Bowl I) three years running from 1965 to 1967, after which Lombardi became general manager and passed the head coach responsibilities on. He had a short stint at the Washington Redskins in 1969, before dying all too soon of cancer in 1970, aged just 57.

As well as being a great coach, Lombardi was a great human being. He openly challenged all forms of discrimination and treated everyone equally and fairly. His teams wouldn't stay in hotels that didn't offer black players the same accommodation as white players, and he openly invited gay players to training camps – all of this at a time when other teams were doing quite the opposite.

He had strong values and impressed these upon the team. He believed strongly in self-awareness, dedication to training and putting the team before the individual. If players let the team down, he was brutally honest with them, but also provided them with the support and coaching to get better. He knew every player's strengths and opportunities for improvement, and got a performance out of everyone.

The NFL trophy now carries his name, the 'Vince Lombardi Trophy', to recognise his achievements as a coach and a human.[1]

IN IT TO WIN IT

Of course, the internet is full of Lombardi quotes, and possibly my two favourites are these:

- 'Individual commitment to a group effort – that is what makes a team work, a company work, a society work, a civilization work.'

- 'People who work together will win, whether it be against complex football defenses, or the problems of modern society.'

The principles and values that Lombardi brought to his teams are equally as applicable to organisations of all sizes in every country around the world. What is often lacking is the leadership qualities required to build a winning team – or else the sense of belonging and togetherness required to achieve the necessary results. Of course, if you have the former, you almost always get the latter, but the latter is still possible if the will and determination is strong.

The same is true of organisations in the private sector and in government. While writing this paragraph I took time off (planned procrastination) to have a coffee and skim-read the news, and one of the main headlines of the news website I was reading was, 'Jacinda Ardern: Political leaders can be both empathetic and strong'. Ardern has rightly won many plaudits over her handling of the Christchurch massacre in 2019, as well as New Zealand's response to the COVID-19 crisis. On both occasions, she demonstrated her individual commitment to a group effort (as Lombardi called it) and did not shy away from making tough decisions and outlining her expectations of the New Zealand people. She was keen for the country to 'win' through on both, whether it was a fight against terrorism and racism or an invisible virus.[2]

The teams that I was part of always wanted to 'win' at whatever it was we were trying to do. Not a 'win at all costs' mentality, but a focus and desire to do the best job that we could and be good humans while we were at it. There are some who believe that winning is bad, or that in order to win you have to go about it in a low EQ way. Both beliefs are wrong.

In her book *Powerful: Building a culture of freedom and responsibility*, author (and former chief talent officer at Netflix) Patty McCord said, 'Winning games is the only measure of success for sports teams, which is why it's not just players but coaches too who are replaced readily on top-performing teams'.

Having internal sports teams is a great way to instil this winning discipline.

A survey of over 2000 workers in the U.K. in 2018 found that competitive sports events were the most popular 'benefit' that organisations could provide to their employees. Over 97 per cent said that they would partake in sports such as football or netball, with mixed-gender teams being more popular than single-sex teams.[3]

The report into the survey findings made three recommendations:

1. Introduce a sports team.
2. Consider signing it up for a challenge.
3. Don't separate by gender.

At this point, it's probably worth saying that team sports don't have to be highly athletic. Remember to ensure that you have a range of activities, or else choose something that doesn't exclude an individual or individuals as a result of their abilities or athletic prowess. Also, you don't want to 'mandate' activities or place undue pressure on anyone to participate: it should always be a choice.

It's no good for your culture or the mental health of your employees if they feel bullied or coerced into doing something. If you've taken the time to define your culture, then people will more readily commit to social activity, as they want to do their bit to be a good teammate. Where they haven't had a say in defining the culture, then they won't feel the need or have the desire to participate. The latter is a failing of the culture, not the individual, so remember to be a good human and exercise some common sense in line with what the team has previously agreed.

Here's a selection of sports teams that I've been part of throughout my career, both single-sex and mixed-gender:

- football (real football, the one the world plays)
- netball
- rounders ('softball' for U.S. readers)
- cycling (this was a 'fun' cycle on exercise bikes for charity)
- basketball
- crown green bowls
- walking
- swimming (again for charity), and
- ten-pin bowling – easily my favourite after the football. We had a great office team that we entered in a league, which we came awfully close to winning!

Individual sports I was part of included:

- darts
- dominoes
- pool
- snooker, and
- table tennis.

Most of these had some form of league arrangement, with different people taking responsibility to organise. With the exception of snooker, all were mixed-gender leagues and you used to really look forward to the draw being made each Monday morning to see who you were playing that week!

MAKE A DAY OF IT

In episode 28 of season 5 of *The Office* (U.S.), fictional paper company Dunder Mifflin holds an office picnic. It's your standard all-company event, with food, entertainment (although Holly and Michael's comedy routine falls flat) and an interdepartmental volleyball tournament. Having re-watched it prior to writing this chapter, the episode's most memorable moment is not when Jim and Pam (played by John Krasinski and Jenna Fischer) find out they're expecting a baby – it's the Idris Elba cameo.

Elba, as character Charles Miner, is part of the corporate team that the Scranton branch (which the focus of the program, if you haven't seen it) have to beat in order to win it all. After some ridiculous delaying tactics, that's exactly what they do. There, you don't need to watch it now. Anyway, the point of the episode is to demonstrate the connection between different employees from different branches of the company, and to introduce a competitive (and fun) element to their coming together.

I've been part of many picnics and sports days and thoroughly enjoyed every one. They all yielded the following benefits:

- **Connection** – I got to meet people that I never would have met and interact with them in a way that helped to develop shared experiences (and stories). The following week I would bump into them in the office and be able to hold a conversation that prior to the sports day wouldn't have been possible.

- **Empathy** – the events provided an opportunity to get to know people in a more relaxed environment, without it feeling forced or uncomfortable. I found out about others' skills, family and background, and even found common ground with many people I had never met before. Mostly, I got to find out about the roles they had and the challenges they faced, which helped to improve empathy across the organisation.

- **Exercise** – depending on the sport we played, the events were always good for a bit of exercise and fresh air. We disconnected from phones, laptops and the work itself to motivate each other to achieve. It was a welcome break from the unhealthy habit of sitting on a chair at a desk for hours on end.

Of course, there are always people who like to take these kinds of days too seriously. I recommend having a planning committee draw up a social contract in advance of the day, so everyone understands what's expected of them. Ensure that there is medical help on hand for the odd sprain, and if you're going to have alcohol and food, better to do it once the event has finished, for obvious reasons!

Team sports are a fantastic way to not only increase collaboration and, therefore, productivity, but also develop a shared sense of wanting to 'win', whatever the task at hand might be.

CULTURE HACK #26:
CREATE A CULTURE CLUB

TL;DR

- Build a cross-functional team of people committed to culture evolution.
- Recognise and reward the best ideas.
- Make the group aspirational.

ONE THING TO STOP

- Seeing culture evolution activities as disconnected training sessions.

I know what you're thinking. 'But Colin, didn't Boy George already do this about 30 years ago?' Well, yes. And no. There's really only one Culture Club and it contained Boy George, Jon Moss, Mikey Craig and Roy Hay. Formed in London in 1981, they're still touring at venues around the world today. I remember seeing them perform 'Do you really want to hurt me' on *Top of the Pops* in the early 80s and loving the mix of new wave and reggae and the way Boy George challenged the traditional view of what a band frontman should look like. It was like nothing I'd ever seen before and the band felt ahead of their time.

Which is a great metaphor for a workplace culture club. It builds on something that's already established, challenges prescribed norms, and looks for ways to be unique or else incrementally improve upon them. It recognises its roots but isn't satisfied staying there.

I've helped organisations around the world implement all of the ideas in the rest of this book via culture club sessions that I run as part of my year-long culture evolution programs. I encourage my clients to maintain their commitment to these events once the program has ended, because once momentum is lost, stagnation sets in and it's hard to get started again.

In my experience, the teams that become exceptional are relentless in their search for better ways to do things. This is the role of the culture club, a cross-functional group of people committed to improving the way things get done.

It has to be cross-functional, because culture is owned by everyone within an organisation, so the club should have representatives from every area. It's not the traditional way of setting up working groups or task forces. Usually their attendees are from the same small group of 'high-potential' employees, rather than having a mix of roles, departments, skill sets, mindsets and ages.

Most organisation cultures are mired in the old ways of doing things and remain in the hands of people who work hard to make change hard. Outdated methods, swim lanes and complex rules serve only to protect the status quo – unless, of course, organisations design and implement something to change that way of thinking and acting.

As Seth Godin said in his book *Tribes: We need you to lead us,* 'Individuals who push their organizations, who inspire other individuals to change the rules, thrive'.

But before we get to that, the culture club has to be something that people want to join.

THE HUMAN POWER OF A COMMUNITY

In his book *Cultivating Communities of Practice: A guide to managing knowledge*, Etienne Wenger said, 'Communities of practice are groups of people who share a concern, a set of problems, or a passion about a topic, and who deepen their knowledge and expertise in this area by interacting on an ongoing basis'. I really like this definition of what it means to be part of something bigger than yourself. Communities of practice are a way to share your experiences, knowledge, failures and feelings to ultimately – and collectively – become better at something with the help of other people who wish to do likewise.

When I moved to New Zealand in 2007, being part of a community was something that I actively sought out. I didn't know anyone at all, so my motivation was to meet people with a shared passion, as I was eager to make an impression in my new job. I was hired because I had a track record of being good with people and teams, but I knew that I didn't have all the answers. So, I looked for opportunities to mix with people with whom I could share my thinking and actions, and who could challenge my biases and assumptions.

Whenever I came across an issue or problem that I felt I couldn't resolve, I would seek out people within the 'community' who could help. They became friends (some of them virtual via Twitter) and we shared a passion to improve the way that things got done. There were healthy debates, good-natured disagreements and a shared commitment to try different things.

With increased access to data via the internet, I was able to research how different organisations built their own communities.

At that time the World Bank was prolific in this space. They had established almost 100 communities (or 'thematics' as they called them) dedicated to sharing knowledge on how to improve social and economic problems from around the world.

If I wasn't able to acquire a skill set required to implement an idea, I would approach the organisation to fund my development. When money was tight (and in government it predominantly was!) then I would pay my own way. I didn't want to stand in the way of my own progress.

This is something I continue today, even though I'm self-employed. Whether it's through the programs that I run or the books that I write, I actively seek out and share the ideas that I glean from others and encourage others to do likewise. I want to ensure that I stay at the forefront of what great culture looks like, so that I can help my clients stay ahead of what's new.

What I learned from the World Bank was that subcultures matter; that the only way to create and maintain a vibrant organisation culture was to ensure that each department and team across the organisation was doing its bit to stay vibrant itself. Spotify does something similar, and then brings its internal communities together to share knowledge and ensure that learning is distributed across the organisation.

At the heart of these culture communities are catalysts: people looking to take accountability for continuous improvement. These are the future leaders of the organisation. They're prepared to discuss, debate and then take action on dumb things that get in the way of change or new things that exploit opportunities. They recognise the power of doing this collaboratively and are deliberate in the way that they form groups. As Thich Nhat Hanh says in his book *The Art of Living,* 'We start with a few colleagues who have the same aspirations, and we build up from there'.

SIMPLE, WELCOMING AND ACTION-ORIENTED

Each group has purpose, participation and progression.

Purpose

Without an understanding of its purpose, the group won't fully grasp the role it exists to fulfil – which is why most internal communities fail to get off the ground. It needs to agree on what the collective passion is, how this connects to the organisation's vision and how they'll spread their word. At this point, it's a community.

If the purpose is easy to digest, then people will want to connect and be part of it. Anything other than that and it will never be accepted and will eventually fail.

Participation

Contrary to what Groucho Marx said, this has to feel like a club that would have you as a member: when you feel part of something, then you contribute. It can't be a club for everyone, as not everyone will have the same shared purpose, but that doesn't mean that it should feel elite in any way. Everyone has an equal say, and while there may be a leader to guide the conversation and outputs, their principal role is to ensure that safety exists and cognitive diversity is encouraged.

A group may have a social contract or a set of principles that members hold themselves to, but if it's welcoming and respectful, that's a great place to start. It also has to have a way to capture ideas or generate content for discussion.

Progression

Gaining commitment from members is one thing, but how do you build momentum? It starts by having a structured program of events through which value is delivered, either to the members of the community or to the organisation. From a member perspective, they should learn new skills or ways of delivering change, while organisational value may be driven through group initiatives.

The group should be encouraged to generate the agenda and share responsibility for community leadership. After all, it's not really a community if everyone doesn't take their turn. People have to be committed regardless of how 'busy' they are, to ensure that momentum is maintained.

Change is going to happen regardless of how stable the culture feels or how well the organisation is doing; by establishing a culture club, you can ensure that 'good enough for now' is never the accepted approach. As Jay Samit said in his book *Disrupt Yourself,* 'History doesn't remember those who maintained the status quo'.

The culture club exists to relentlessly create a new status quo and a new generation of leaders whose aim is to ensure that the organisation is always fit for the future of work. That is the legacy opportunity for everyone involved.

Cultural evolution needs to be a continual priority, and with courage, determination, collaboration, drive and a few crazy ideas, everything could change, forever.

I've given you 26 ideas in this book. The rest is up to you.

THANKS

As with all of my books, I'd like to thank my family for providing me with the time and space to devote to my writing. This time was different to the previous four, as instead of writing the book in hotels, airport lounges, cafes, offices and in the air, I wrote it all at home, due to the isolation orders imposed as a result of the COVID-19 virus. Apologies for continually dipping in and out of the family activities we created to maintain our sanity!

I'd like to thank my friend Dom Price for the continued laughs, inspiration and his sage advice. The 'One thing to stop' idea was his and I immediately incorporated it into the book. If only he wasn't from Manchester…

And thanks to my U.S. brother Rick Morris for being there when I needed someone to talk to. Oh, and for taking the piss out of me. Cheers for that, too.

I'd also like to thank every single person who has supported me on my journey so far. These include:

- people who put their trust in me to deliver in the early days (and today!), when they hadn't really heard of me or the work that I did

- people who influenced their management teams to spend money on culture development or project-management improvement when it's typically not something that they spent money on

- anyone, anywhere who has ever read, liked, shared or commented on a blog that I've written (even if you didn't like it!)

- people who have religiously turned up to events that I've organised or been part of, or who have watched the videos I've put out into the world

- everyone who has bought one of my other books (and you for buying this one!), and

- every member of the Culture Fix Community (culturefixcommunity.com) who has actively engaged in making it what it is today, and also those members of the Inner Circle who provide content ideas for me to develop on their behalf!

This is the fifth book I've written in five years, and if it weren't for everyone listed above, I'd never have written one. Thank you so much for your continued support.

ABOUT THE AUTHOR

Colin D. Ellis is an international award-winning public speaker, a facilitator of culture and project-management programs and author of four bestselling books. (He's hoping this will be the fifth.) He's not great at writing in the third person but will give it a go and may overdo the self-deprecation in the process.

Colin was born at a very early age in the Liverpool suburb of Whiston (about eight miles east of the centre, to be precise) to David and Freda. He was the eldest of three boys. He grew up in the neighbouring village of Rainhill with a love for Everton Football Club – still the only football team (worth supporting) in Liverpool – and in his teenage years, music (which he listened to, but never played).

He can't remember how much of this he's written in other books, so he's going to try to write some different things as he can't be bothered to go and check.

He lived at home until he was 23, because he didn't get the grades to go to university and it was easier and cheaper than buying a house of his own. He squandered the extra money he had on drinking cheap lager and going on foreign holidays with his friends, and is glad that those days are behind him because he drinks whisky now.

His life changed in 1997 when he was asked to become a project manager to help fix the Y2K problem in the organisation he was working for at that time. He loved building teams and never stopped looking for ways to evolve his management style, by writing down the things he liked (and didn't) in others.

This is turning into *This is Your Life* now, so he'll try and wrap it up.

He emigrated to New Zealand with his family in 2007 and brought his crazy ideas about team culture and project delivery to government there, having previously spent all his career in the private sector. Some things worked, some things didn't, but that didn't stop him trying.

Australia called in 2013 and Melbourne has been his home since then, with his wife and two teenage children. He started to work for himself in 2015 and for the first six months it was rubbish. Things were so bad he almost had to move back home to live with family in England (aged 46). No-one seemed to want commonsense approaches or for their staff to be taught how to do things for themselves, but he kept at it and six months later, with three clients, he started to get some traction. He has worked bloody hard to maintain that momentum ever since.

In short, he helps organisations to create cultural legacies by teaching their people how to be the best versions of themselves and how to build and maintain vibrancy, productivity and accountability in the way they do things. He also makes sure there are plenty of laughs, because without laughter there's no sunshine in the house.

If that's not enough information, then you can find out more about Colin's work by heading to colindellis.com.

SOUNDTRACK

Music is my salvation while writing, so it's only right that I list the artists and their albums that I listened to during the eight weeks it took me to research and write this book. I struggled (from a mental-health perspective) during the COVID-19 crisis, so I ended up revisiting many albums that I listened to when I was younger, as I felt safer there. So, for those of you who liked this section in my other books, you will notice more 80s and 90s music than you would normally!

A Flock of Seagulls – *The Best Of*

ABC – *The Lexicon of Love*

A-ha – *Scoundrel Days*

Black – *Wonderful Life*

Blur – *Parklife*

Bronski Beat – *The Age of Consent*

Carter U.S.M. – *30 Something*

China Crisis – *Flaunt the Imperfection*

City Calm Down – *Echoes in Blue*

Deacon Blue – *Our Town: The Greatest Hits*

Donald Glover – *3.15.20*

Echo & the Bunnymen – *Songs to Learn & Sing*

Howard Jones – *Human's Lib*

John Williams – *Harry Potter and the Prisoner of Azkaban*

John Williams – *Star Wars: Episode IV Original Soundtrack*

Kingmaker – *Sleepwalking*

Kraftwerk – *The Man-Machine*

London Grammar – *Truth is a Beautiful Thing*

Morrissey – *I am not a Dog on a Chain*

Oasis – *Definitely Maybe*

Pet Shop Boys – *Discography*

Public Service Broadcasting – *Every Valley*

Public Service Broadcasting – *The Race for Space*

Pulp – *Different Class*

Puressence – *Only Forever*

Radiohead – *Pablo Honey*

Radiohead – *OK Computer*

Red Rum Club – *Matador*

Scritti Politti – *Cupid & Psyche 85*

Shack – *H.M.S. Fable*

Shed Seven – *Going for Gold*

Strangelove – *Time for the Rest of Our Lives*

Supergrass – *I Should Coco*

Tchaikovsky – The Ballet Suites

Tears for Fears – *The Hurting*

The Beautiful South – *Welcome to the Beautiful South*

The Beautiful South – *0898 Beautiful South*

The Beta Band – *The Best Of*

The Courteeners – *More. Again. Forever.*

The Dears – *Lovers Rock*

The Electric Soft Parade – *Holes in the Wall*

The La's – *The La's*

The Real People – *The Real People*

The Smiths – *Meat is Murder*

The Smiths – *The Queen is Dead*

The Smiths – *Strangeways, Here We Come*

The Weeknd – *After Hours*

The Wonder Stuff – *Construction for the Modern Idiot*

The Wonder Stuff – *Never Loved Elvis*

Thompson Twins – *The Collection*

Tim Burgess – *I Love the New Sky*

ENDNOTES

Culture Hack #1

1. en.wikipedia.org/wiki/Ray_Tomlinson
2. phrasee.co/a-brief-history-of-email/
3. en.wikipedia.org/wiki/You%27ve_Got_Mail
4. cnbc.com/2019/04/18/nigerian-prince-scams-still-rake-in-over-700000-dollars-a-year.html
5. atlassian.com/time-wasting-at-work-infographic
6. radicati.com/wp/wp-content/uploads/2018/12/Email-Statistics-Report-2019-2023-Executive-Summary.pdf
7. journals.aom.org/doi/10.5465/AMBPP.2018.121
8. Quoted in *TIME Mental Health: A new understanding*, 2018.
9. on.ft.com/2Gq8aNY
10. en.wikipedia.org/wiki/Right_to_disconnect
11. atlassian.com/time-wasting-at-work-infographic
12. atlassian.com/time-wasting-at-work-infographic

Culture Hack #2

1. variety.com/2017/digital/news/netflix-company-culture-document-1202474529/
2. ftms.edu.my/images/Document/MOD003554%20-%20Effective%20Team%20and%20Performance%20Management/WEEK%205_Druskat%20Wolff%20(2008)_EI%20of%20teams.pdf
3. infed.org/mobi/bruce-w-tuckman-forming-storming-norming-and-performing-in-groups/
4. atlassian.com/blog/teamwork/team-productivity-tips-and-research

Culture Hack #3

1. nytimes.com/2017/07/21/science/procrastination-research-conference.html
2. pmi.org/about/press-media/press-releases/2018-pulse-of-the-profession-survey

3. thecut.com/2017/07/one-in-five-people-are-chronic-procrastinators.html

4. nature.com/articles/srep33203

5. bustle.com/p/what-procrastinating-looks-like-in-your-brain-according-to-experts-18538249

6. neuroscientificallychallenged.com/blog/2014/5/16/know-your-brain-prefrontal-cortex

7. static1.squarespace.com/static/5b7692e636099b2247325aea/t/5bade857f9619a3ac9b1b83c/1538123866021/8-week+Mindfulness+Based+Stress+Reduction+induces+brain+changes.pdf

8. scifi.stackexchange.com/questions/25208/why-did-c-3po-close-down-while-luke-talked-to-ben-in-a-new-hope

Culture Hack #4

1. atlassian.com/time-wasting-at-work-infographic

2. bit.ly/2IVt48I

Culture Hack #5

1. britannica.com/biography/Inigo-Jones

2. biography.yourdictionary.com/inigo-jones

3. hrp.org.uk/banqueting-house/whats-on/banqueting-hall/#gs.6aqle0

4. londongrandtour.wordpress.com/2010/12/11/inigo-jones-the-original-grand-tourist/

5. blog.crisp.se/wp-content/uploads/2014/03/unproject.pdf

Culture Hack #6

1. aytm.com/surveys/348518/stat/2477ab127d36c062e5fcb3c1a8990796#charts

2. news.bbc.co.uk/2/hi/8689010.stm

3. shmaltzandmenudo.wordpress.com/2016/06/12/famous-sayings-14-honesty-is-the-best-policy/

4. apa.org/news/press/releases/2012/08/lying-less

5. hbr.org/2014/07/the-skills-leaders-need-at-every-level

6. psychologytoday.com/us/blog/emotional-fitness/201411/honesty-can-make-or-break-relationship

7. honesteddie.com/comsky_ltr.html

8. hbr.org/2011/03/dont-be-nice-be-helpful

9. en.wikipedia.org/wiki/Honesty_Day

Culture Hack #7

1. theguardian.com/uk-news/2020/mar/20/scottish-hotel-sacks-12-staff-over-coronavirus-making-them-homeless
2. twitter.com/andyinverness/status/1240742756810665997
3. pwc.com/us/en/library/workforce-of-the-future/fulfillment-at-work.html
4. liverpoolecho.co.uk/news/liverpool-news/britannia-hotels-blames-brutal-coronavirus-17953497
5. twitter.com/afneil/status/1240895962144550914
6. gallup.com/workplace/236366/right-culture-not-employee-satisfaction.aspx

Culture Hack #8

1. foundr.com/onboarding-best-practices/
2. gallup.com/workplace/235121/why-onboarding-experience-key-retention.aspx
3. techfestconf.com/ld-aus/blog-1/the-power-of-play-how-the-lego-group-has-built-fun-into-their-employee-experience
4. zapier.com/about/
5. zapier.com/learn/remote-work/remote-job-hunting/
6. themuse.com/advice/the-ultimate-guide-to-researching-a-company-preinterview
7. zapier.com/jobs/our-commitment-to-applicants/
8. linkedin.com/posts/piquette-%26-howard-electric-service-inc-_worksafelivesafe-phelectric2020-newphemployeeswag-activity-6666709906068000768-Qgzw

Culture Hack #9

1. ted.com/talks/astro_teller_the_unexpected_benefit_of_celebrating_failure?language=en
2. psychologytoday.com/au/blog/the-gen-y-guide/201705/is-what-happens-your-brain-when-you-fail
3. hbr.org/2012/01/positive-intelligence
4. journals.sagepub.com/doi/10.1177/0956797616639727
5. sciencedirect.com/science/article/pii/S0065260106380021
6. cnbc.com/id/46101756
7. breakpointbook.com/jeff-stibel-creator-of-the-failure-wall-takes-on-the-greatest-failures-of-all/
8. i0.wp.com/www.breakpointbook.com/wp-content/uploads/2015/01/img_9144.jpg

9. afr.com/work-and-careers/management/10-questions-with-google-australia-boss-melanie-silva-20190220-h1bi9h

10. mindful.org/why-vulnerability-is-your-superpower/

Culture Hack #10

1. en.wikipedia.org/wiki/Ink_and_Incapability

2. atlasobscura.com/articles/1700s-book-clubs-drinking-socializing

3. en.wikipedia.org/wiki/Benjamin_Franklin

4. jstor.org/stable/3594275?seq=1

5. usatoday30.usatoday.com/life/books/news/2011-05-22-Oprah-Winfrey-Book-Club_n.htm

6. usatoday30.usatoday.com/life/books/news/2011-05-22-Oprah-Winfrey-Book-Club_n.htm

7. en.wikipedia.org/wiki/Book_Club_(film)

Culture Hack #11

1. pubmed.ncbi.nlm.nih.gov/19367130/

2. thedelite.com/celebrities-with-weird-wonderful-hobbies/18/

3. pwc.com/us/en/library/workforce-of-the-future/fulfillment-at-work.html

4. ncbi.nlm.nih.gov/pmc/articles/PMC2863117/

5. onlinelibrary.wiley.com/doi/abs/10.1111/joop.12064

6. en.wikipedia.org/wiki/Arthur_Lydiard

7. healthdirect.gov.au/neuromuscular-system

8. thesportjournal.org/article/tools-and-benefits-of-periodization-developing-an-annual-training-plan-and-promoting-performance-improvements-in-athletes/

9. en.wikipedia.org/wiki/Roger_Bannister

10. en.wikipedia.org/wiki/Jogging

11. news.google.com/newspapers?id=T7pQAAAAIBAJ&sjid=OOMDAAAAIBAJ&pg=2989%2C558389

12. statista.com/topics/1743/running-and-jogging/

Culture Hack #12

1. online.king.edu/news/cell-phone-addiction/

2. mobilecoach.com/8-surprising-cell-phone-statistics/

3. drive.google.com/file/d/0B9W_ZHUehuLcUUhnSVZsSE5VT2M/view

4. kwhs.wharton.upenn.edu/2019/06/take-cell-phone-bed/

5. journals.sagepub.com/doi/abs/10.1111/j.1468-2982.2008.01714.x

6. pubmed.ncbi.nlm.nih.gov/30774207/?from_linkname=pubmed_pubmed_reviews&from_from_uid=30774207&from_single_result_display=pubmed_pubmed_reviews+for+PMID%3A+30774207

7. study.com/academy/lesson/thorax-definition-and-anatomy.html

8. physio-pedia.com/Forward_Head_Posture

9. en.wikipedia.org/wiki/IHunch

10. en.wikipedia.org/wiki/Hindu_philosophy

11. healthiestworkplace.aia.com/australia/eng/

12. journals.lww.com/joem/Abstract/2017/03000/Employer_and_Employee_Opinions_About_Workplace.4.aspx

13. www2.deloitte.com/global/en/pages/about-deloitte/articles/millennialsurvey.html

14. monster.com/career-advice/article/companies-good-wellness-programs

15. risepeople.com/blog/workplace-wellness-programs/

Culture Hack #13

1. forbes.com/sites/stevedenning/2019/05/23/understanding-fake-agile/#555c78574bbe

2. hbr.org/2016/09/excess-management-is-costing-the-us-3-trillion-per-year

3. ronjeffries.com/articles/018-01ff/abandon-1/

4. medium.com/@coleharper/implementing-googles-bureaucracy-busters-initiative-bb922138d012

Culture Hack #14

1. *A Social History of England*, 900–1200, edited by Julia Crick and Elisabeth van Houts, Cambridge University Press, 2001.

2. en.wikipedia.org/wiki/Board_game

3. discoveringegypt.com/ancient-egyptian-game-senet/

4. ancient-origins.net/artifacts-other-artifacts/fun-everyone-evolving-history-board-games-007250

5. chessvariants.com/history.html

6. en.wikipedia.org/wiki/Chess

7. brandonthegamedev.com/the-10-most-popular-board-games-of-all-time-and-why-they-made-board-gaming-better/

8. qz.com/250667/chess-players-are-dying-in-the-middle-of-competitive-matches/

9. bbc.com/news/magazine-26328105

10. theguardian.com/games/2019/nov/29/gamers-back-under-dungeons-and-dragons-spell

11. howgameareyou.com/health-benefits-board-games/

12. investor.realnetworks.com/press-releases/press-release-details/2006/Research-Reveals-Casual-Games-Provide-Mental-Balance-Stress-Relief-and-Relaxation/default.aspx

Culture Hack #15

1. nytimes.com/2016/08/09/podcasts/introducing-the-run-up-our-new-election-podcast.html

2. nymag.com/intelligencer/2020/01/michael-barbaro-the-daily-podcast-new-york-times.html

3. en.wikipedia.org/wiki/Juice_(aggregator)

4. computer.howstuffworks.com/internet/basics/podcasting1.htm

5. edisonresearch.com/the-infinite-dial-2020/

Culture Hack #16

1. en.wikipedia.org/wiki/Year_2000_problem

2. en.wikipedia.org/wiki/Year_2000_problem

3. agilemanifesto.org/history.html

4. thedigitalprojectmanager.com/scrum-ceremonies-made-simple/

5. atlassian.com/agile/scrum/ceremonies

6. shreedamani.wordpress.com/2013/04/29/agile-showcases-guide-to-effective-showcase/

7. medium.com/@kartik.narayanan/agile-showcases-d9890205bf8b

Culture Hack #17

1. britannica.com/place/Tel-Aviv-Yafo/History

2. en.wikipedia.org/wiki/1921_Jaffa_riots

3. en.wikipedia.org/wiki/Winston_Churchill

4. en.wikipedia.org/wiki/Balfour_Declaration

5. theguardian.com/careandsupportreform/what-green-paper

6. en.wikipedia.org/wiki/White_paper

7. foleon.com/topics/how-to-write-and-format-a-white-paper

8. diggintravel.com/airasia-digital-airline/

9. economictimes.indiatimes.com/magazines/panache/airasia-boss-signs-out-of-twitter-calls-social-media-an-angry-place/articleshow/73316907.cms?from=mdr

10. chrisfharvey.com/2012/11/tony-fernandes-dream-the-impossible/

11. issuu.com/airasia/docs/7-july_2012

12. leaderonomics.com/personal/crowdsourcing-a-new-paradigm-of-knowledge-management

Culture Hack #18

1. media.the-ceo-magazine.com/guest/ceo-visibility-–-new-dimension-branding
2. cnbc.com/2019/11/11/airbnb-ceo-brian-chesky-what-caused-weworks-fall.html
3. psychology.illinoisstate.edu/ktschne/psy376/Hogan_Kaiser.pdf
4. phrases.org.uk/meanings/fish-rot-from-the-head-down.html
5. virgin.com/entrepreneur/richard-branson-world-needs-more-kind-and-considerate-leaders
6. *Work Rules: Insights from inside Google that will transform how you live and lead* by Laszlo Bock, John Murray, 2015.
7. fastcompany.com/90213545/exclusive-spotify-ceo-daniel-ek-on-apple-facebook-netflix-and-the-future-of-music
8. braintrustceo.com/blog-posts/top-5-ways-ceos-can-increase-visibility-2019/

Culture Hack #19

1. telegraph.co.uk/culture/theatre/theatre-news/11600295/Jim-Dale-Interview-I-wasnt-good-friends-with-the-carry-on-clique.html
2. gizmodo.com.au/2016/09/melbournes-imax-screen-is-now-the-worlds-largest-because-sydneys-is-gone/
3. bluebulbprojects.com/MeasureOfThings/results.php?p=1&comp=height&unit=m&amt=32&sort=pr
4. goodtherapy.org/learn-about-therapy/types/movie-therapy
5. telegraph.co.uk/news/health/3330249/Movie-therapy-Do-you-believe-in-the-healing-power-of-film.html
6. psychcentral.com/blog/cinematherapy-the-healing-power-of-movies-and-tv/
7. telegraph.co.uk/news/health/3330249/Movie-therapy-Do-you-believe-in-the-healing-power-of-film.html
8. en.wikipedia.org/wiki/The_Day_After_Tomorrow
9. heguardian.com/culture/2020/mar/19/netflix-party-could-this-group-watching-tech-gimmick-be-a-lifesaver

Culture Hack #21

1. dcau.fandom.com/wiki/List_of_times_Superman_saved_Lois_Lane_in_the_DCAU
2. cbr.com/times-lois-saved-superman/

3. theguardian.com/global-development/poverty-matters/2014/oct/22/ethiopian-famine-report-influence-modern-coverage

4. en.wikipedia.org/wiki/Bob_Geldof

5. en.wikipedia.org/wiki/Do_They_Know_It%27s_Christmas%3F

6. en.wikipedia.org/wiki/Band_Aid_(band)

7. library.glassdoor.com/c/millennials-vs-gen-z?x=hRe2tY

8. shrm.org/hr-today/trends-and-forecasting/research-and-surveys/Documents/2018%20Employee%20Benefits%20Report.pdf

9. salesforce.org/philanthropy-cloud-overview/giving-your-workforce-a-voice-download/

10. peterbaines.com.au/new-blog/2016/7/18/why-giving-your-staff-one-day-off-a-year-to-volunteer-is-not-working

11. fsprivatewealth.com.au/media/library/FS_PrivateWealth/Misc/FS_Private_Wealth__A_Snapshot_of_Australian_Giving.pdf?9a82c

12. outbackteambuilding.com/team-building/end-hunger-games/

Culture Hack #22

1. businessinsider.com/shopify-ceo-success-long-hours-40-hour-week-2019-12

2. kronos.com/resource/download/23811

3. psychologicalscience.org/observer/burnout-and-the-brain

4. habitsforwellbeing.com/the-12-phases-of-burnout-according-to-psychologists/

5. itrevolution.com/understanding-job-burnout-christina-maslach/

6. thecie.com.au/wp-content/uploads/2016/04/Economic-value-of-pathology_-Final-Report-April-2016.pdf

7. cipd.co.uk/Images/health-and-well-being-2020-report_tcm18-73967.pdf

8. businessinsider.com/shopify-ceo-success-long-hours-40-hour-week-2019-12

9. fastcompany.com/1300971/cisco-says-telecommuting-saves-money-and-world

10. atlassian.com/teamwork/artificial-intelligence

Culture Hack #23

1. en.wikipedia.org/wiki/Greensboro,_North_Carolina

2. linkedin.com/company/center-for-creative-leadership

3. ccl.org/articles/leading-effectively-articles/70-20-10-rule/

4. kornferry.com/insights/articles/job-hunting-2018-boredom

5. gallup.com/workplace/238085/state-american-workplace-report-2017.aspx

6. fastcompany.com/90213545/exclusive-spotify-ceo-daniel-ek-on-apple-facebook-netflix-and-the-future-of-music

Culture Hack #24

1. abcnews.go.com/Travel/fear-flying-good-things/story?id=20471481
2. elitedaily.com/news/world/people-terrified-plane-crashes-even-though-rare/977885
3. en.wikipedia.org/wiki/Pre-flight_safety_demonstration#History_of_Pre-Recorded_Safety_Videos
4. citylab.com/life/2017/12/the-evolution-of-airline-safety-videos/548858/
5. vimeo.com/59511729
6. youtu.be/qOw44VFNk8Y
7. fiercevideo.com/video/video-will-account-for-82-all-internet-traffic-by-2022-cisco-says
8. youtube.com/watch?v=jNQXAC9IVRw
9. engadget.com/2016-11-10-the-history-of-youtube.html
10. timesofisrael.com/internship-film-focuses-on-googles-good-side/

Culture Hack #25

1. en.wikipedia.org/wiki/Vince_Lombardi
2. theguardian.com/world/2020/may/31/jacinda-ardern-political-leaders-can-be-both-empathetic-and-strong
3. perkbox.com/uk/resources/library/interactive-the-great-perk-search

INDEX

80-hour work week 172

A Room With a View 46
Academy of Management, The 15
accessibility 122
accountability 56
Advanced Research Projects Agency
    Network (ARPANET) 14
Agile 48
Agile Manifesto 107, 128
agility 105-106, 129
AirAsia 137-138
Airbnb offsites 155-162
Alfred the Great 112
Alter, Adam 18
Amazon 48, 166
Amazon Prime 153
America Online (AOL) 14
American football 194
Amsterdam 156
amygdala 31, 33
Angela's Ashes 85
Apple 166
Apple Podcasts 122
Ardern, Jacinda 197
Arrival 151
Art of Living, The 35
Asana 101
Atkinson, Rowan 80
Atlantic, The 83
Atlassian 49
Atomic Habits 181
attraction 123

Australian Financial Review 79
Avengers: Infinity War 84
AYTM 51

Baines, Peter 168
Bannister, Sir Roger 92
Barbaro, Michael 118-119
Baruch, R. 150
behaviour 27
belonging 28, 67
Berg-Cross, L. 150
Bergen, Candice 84
Berkeley 173
Bernini, Gian Lorenzo 46
bias 160
Blackadder 80-81
BlackBerry 18
board games 111-117
Bombeck, Emma 83
Book Club 83
book clubs, benefits of 86
book groups 80-87
book lists 84
boredom 181, 183
Boston University Questrom School
    of Business 172
Bowerman, Bill 92, 93
Brain and Cognition 33
BRAIN program 138
Branson, Richard 144
Bridgewater Associates 62, 108
Britannia Hotels 59-61, 65

British Association for Counselling and Psychotherapy 151
Brown, Brené 79
brown-bag lunch 131
Brydon, Rob 46
Buerk, Michael 164
building connection 62
building teams 23
bureaucracy 103-110
Bureaucracy Busters 108-109
burnout 172-174
Burson-Marsteller 142
business as usual (BAU) 8-9
busting bureaucracy, benefits of 108
busyness 9, 32

Canva 139
capability 168
Caravaggio, Michelangelo Merisi da 46
Cards Against Humanity 112
Carrey, Jim 89
Carry On movies 148-149
Catmull, Ed 7
Center for Creative Leadership (CCL) 179-180
CEOs 142-143, 145-147
Chang, Do Won 142
change 45, 207
Chaplin, Charlie 77
Chartered Institute of Personnel and Development (CIPD) 174
chatting with the chief 140-147
Chesky, Brian 143
chess 112-114
Chicago White Sox 53, 54
children's hospital, Perth, WA 38-39
Christchurch massacre 197
chronic procrastinator 30, 32
Churchill, Winston 134
Cincinnati Reds 54
cinema therapy 150

Cisco 101, 166, 175, 189
clarity 32
Clean Up Australia 168
Clear, James 181
Clinton, Hillary 118
CNBC 14
coaching 186
code of conduct 85
cognitive skills 116
collaboration 27, 72, 153
collaboration tools 2, 176
Coltrane, Robbie 80
combatant cultures 106
Comiskey, Charles 54
command and control 2, 127-128, 129
commitment 162
communication 13, 26, 56, 61, 63, 183, 186,
community 49, 50, 70
community of learning 84-86
compact discs 120
computer use 96
confidence 91
connection 167, 200
consumerisation 95
continual learning 74, 84
Coogan, Steve 46
Corrections, The 83
Covent Garden 45, 47
COVID-19 7, 8-9, 42, 59, 71, 114, 115, 153, 175, 197
Coylumbridge Hotel 59
creative thinking 4
creativity 37, 44, 91
Creativity, Inc. 7
Crothall, Marc 60
Crowley, Dermot 40
Crusade, The 113
Cultivating Communities of Practice: A guide to managing knowledge 204
cultural evolution 8, 94, 183, 207

Culture Amp 49, 62
culture club 202-207
culture decks 21-22
culture definition 185
culture enhancement 117
Culture Fix Community 50
Culture Fix: How to create a great place to work 5, 15, 26
Culture Makers 12, 62, 121
culture starts at the top 142-143
culture videos 187-193
Curry, Adam 120
Curtis, Richard 80
Customer Champion roles 69

Daily Telegraph 149
Daily, The 119
Daimler 15
Dalai Lama 35
Dale, Jim 149
Dalio, Ray 25, 62, 108
Deadpool 2 84
decision-making 31, 37
DeGeneres, Ellen 76
deliberate action 26
Deloitte Global Millennial survey 100
Denning, Steve 105
DePaul University 29
Design Thinking Methodology 64
digestion 99
discipline 178
disengagement, cost of 182
Disney+ 153
Dr Seuss 85
Dropbox 190
Druskat, V.A. 22
Dun & Bradstreet Credibility Corporation 76
Dun & Bradstreet failure wall 77
Dungeons & Dragons 114
Dweck, Carol 74

Edison Research 121
Edison, Thomas 77
Eichinger, Robert A. 179, 185
Ek, Daniel 146, 183
Elon Musk 17, 42
Elton, Ben 80, 81
Elzinga, Didier 62
email 13-20
Emanuel, Ari 98
Emotional Capitalists 34
emotions 31
empathy 143, 167, 200
empathy mapping 63-64
employee-engagement 156
engagement 48
engagement surveys 143
entertainment 153, 161
Ethiopia 164
Europae Speculum 52
Everton FC 112, 126
exercise 200
expectations, setting 177, 186

Facebook 51, 138
facilitators 160-161
failing visibly 73-79
Failure Wall, The 77
fear 31
feedback 56-57, 130, 196
Feingersh, Seth 122
Feng, Tingyong 31
Fernandes, Tony 137
Ferrari, Dr Joseph 29, 30
field trips 45-50
FIFA 34
Fifty Shades of Grey 83
financial advice 102
financial health 70
Fischer, Bobby 114
flexible working 8-9, 100, 175-178
Florence 46
focus 99

Fonda, Jane 83
Forbes 105
Fordham University 194
Forever 21 142
forward head posture (FHP) 96-97
Four Seconds 56
France 16
Frankenstein 46
Franklin, Benjamin 81
Franzen, Jonathan 83
Freedom 83
Freudenberger, Herbert J. 172
fun 116, 123

Gallup *62, 67, 182*
Gallup survey 147
Gandil, Chick 54
Garcia, Andy 84
Geldof, Bob 164-165
Gen Z 166
Glassdoor survey 166
goal setting 186
goals, group 23
goals, individual 23
Godin, Seth 203
Goethe, Johann Wolfgang von 46
Goldberg, M. Hirsh 57
Good Idea Club 137
Google 35, 73, 79, 108, 144, 190
Google Chrome 153
governance 108
Grand Tour 46
Grease 149
Green Bay Packers 195
green papers 134-135
group dynamics 23
group identity 22
growth 75

Haimovitz, Kyla 74
Hanh, Thich Nhat 35, 205
Hanks, Tom 14, 89

happiness 28
Harris, W.E. 93
Harvard Business Review 56
HBR Guide to Leading Teams 61
health 144
healthcare 192
Herron, Jerry S. 82
hobbies 90-92
– benefits of 91
hobby expos 87-94
Hodson, Phillip 151
Hoffman, Reid 73
Hogan, Robert 143
honest conversations 5
honesty 51-56
Honesty Day 57
Hsieh, Tony 48
humanity 122
humour 4

IBM 138
IDEO 49
iHunch 97
IMAX 150
inducting employees 66-72
Innocents Abroad, The 46
innovation 9, 27, 77-78, 184
innovation hubs 2
Innovation Jam 138
inspiration 72
Instagram 32
interacting 152
interview process 68, 69, 70-71
ipods 119, 120
IQ 19
*Irresistible: The Rise of Addictive
    Technology and the Business of
    Keeping Us Hooked* 18
Italian Journey 46

Jackson, Janet 190
Jeffries, Ron 107

Jennings, P. 150
job rotation 182-183, 185
job swaps 179-186
Jogging 93
Johnson, Don 84
Johnson, Samuel 80, 81
Jones, Inigo 45, 46, 47
Jordan, Michael 77
Journal of Occupational and
  Organizational Psychology 91
JPMorgan Chase 166
Jung, Carl 63
Junto 81, 82
Jurassic Park 151

Kaiser, Robert B. 143
Kalanick, Travis 142
Karpov, Anatoly 114
Keaton, Diane 84
Kennedy, Robert F. 77
Kniberg, Henrik 48
Knight, Phil 93
knitting 89
Korn Ferry 181
Krishnaji, Sri 98

Lane, Lois 164
law of the customer 105-106
leadership 38, 72, 144, 156
leadership library 80
learning 73-74, 75, 91, 152
LEGO Group 68-69
Leonardo da Vinci 46
LinkedIn 50, 71, 72, 73, 183
literary clubs 81
Live Aid 165
Liverpool Echo 61, 126-127
Lobban, Bill 59
Lombardi, Vince T. 194-196
Lombardo, Michael M. 179, 185
London 45
loyalty 168

Lütke, Tobi 171, 174
Lydiard, Arthur Leslie 92

MAILBOX 14
Mann, Leslie 89
Maslach, Christina 173
massage 101
McCall, Morgan 179, 185
McChrystal, General Stanley 38
McCord, Patty 198
Medici family 46
meditation 34-36, 97, 98
meeting management 41-42
meetings 37-44
– planning 40-41
– virtual 42
Menlo Innovations 44
mental health 198
mentoring 186
Michelangelo 46
Microsoft 100-101
Millennials 95, 166
Millennium Bug 126
mindfulness 35
mindset 74, 158
Monzon, Merriliz Rivera 97, 98, 99
motivation 72
movie nights 148-154
–benefits of 152-153
Murphy, John Edward 53-55
Muse, The 69
Musk, Elon 42

National Lampoon's European
  Vacation 46
Nature 31
neck pain 96
Neil, Andrew 61
Nelson, Craig T. 84
Netflix 21-22, 48, 153, 198
Netflix Parties 148, 153, 154
network, the law of 106

networking 49
Neumann, Adam 142
New York Giants 53, 195
New York Times 35, 79, 118, 119, 143
New Zealand 197, 204
New Zealand Herald 92
Newman, Martyn 34
Nietzsche, Friedrich 74
Nike 93, 94

O&O Academy 98
offsites 155, 157, 159
onboarding 66-72
open-plan offices 1
Oprah's Book Club 83
out-of-office messages 16

Palestine 133, 134
Palladio, Andrea 46
participation 206
Patagonia 98
PayPal 189
PechaKucha 44
performance 144, 184
performance training 92
periodisation 92
personality 26
personality types 63
Peter Bregman 56
Philadelphia Athletics 53
Pichette, Patrick 108
Picquette & Howard Electric Service
    Inc. 71
Pitt, Brad 90
Pixar 95
planning for perfection 75
podcasts 118-124
podcasts, US 118-119
poor performance 2, 9
posture 99
*Powerful: Building a culture of freedom
    and responsibility* 198

PowerPoint 139
Preethaji, Sri 98
prefrontal cortex 31, 32
presentations 125
presenteeism 172
Principles 25, 62, 108
problem-solving 74
procrastination 29-36
Procrastination Conference 30
productive work 172
productivity 26, 181
professional development 179, 180
professional services company 60
progression 206-207
Project Management Institute 30
Psychological Bulletin 23
Psychology Today 53, 74
Psychosomatic Medicine 90
Public Accounts Committee 38-39
purpose 3, 206
purpose statements 166
PwC 60, 90

Queen Nefertari 112

Radicati Group, The 15
recognition 163
recruiting 68
Register-Guard 93
relationship-building 116
reluctance 160
Renaissance, the 45
reputation 122, 167
resilience 183
respect 160
revenue 122
'right to disconnect' laws 16
risk, managing 187-188
risk-taking 76-77
Roberts, Julia 89
Rothstein, Arnold 54
routines, establishing 177

Rowling, J.K. 113
Royal College of Psychiatrists 150
Rubens, Peter Paul 46
Rumi 143
Runner's World 92
running clubs 92-94
running, benefits of 93
Run-up, The 118
Ryan, Meg 14
Ryder, Leah 26

safety 56-57, 78, 144
Sandberg, Sheryl 51
Sandys, Sir Edwin 52
Sarandon, Susan 89
Science Museum in London 52
Science of Honesty study 53
Scotland 59
Scottish Tourism Alliance 60
Scrum methodology 42
Search Inside Yourself 35
Searls, Doc 121
self-awareness 79
self-control 31
self-esteem 91
Senet 112
Shakespeare, William 52
Shapiro, Mary 61
SharePoint 49
Sheahan, Casey 98
Shelley, Mary 46
Shopify 171, 174
showcases 125-132
Silva, Melanie 79
Simplicity Circle 109
Simpsons, The 126
small team, the law of 106
Smart Teams 40
Smartphones 18
Smith, Will 90
socialising 152
Sony Walkman 120

Southwest Airlines 191
sports 198-199
sports days 194-201
sports teams 199
Spotify 48-49, 76, 122, 146, 182
staff turnover 66
stakeholder engagement 64-65
stakeholders, managing 58-65
Star Wars 35, 149, 150
start-up, think like a 107
Steenburgen, Mary 84
Stibel, Jeff 76, 77
storytelling 192
Stossel, Scott 83
Stranger Things 114
strategy 2, 159
stress 32, 98, 116
stretching 95-102
subcultures 205
subjective discomfort 30
succession planning 184
Super Bowl 190, 196
Surf Life Saving New South Wales 168
Swift, Taylor 90

Tan, Chade-Meng 35
team culture 4
Team of Teams 38
team-building 154, 155, 156
teamwork 21-28
technical systems 125
technology 8
TED talks 36, 84
Teller, Astro 73
telling lies 52
Tesla 17
The Art of Living 205
The Book of Lies 57
The Empire Strikes Back 151
The Hobbit 189
The Internship 190
The Office 200

The Quibbler 193
The Road 85
The Social Network 190
The Trip to Italy 46
Thomson, Andrew 59
threats 31
Titian 46
Tomlinson, Ray 14
town hall meetings 146
Toy Story 3 151
Toyota 137
training 1
trainspotting 87-89
Trello 26
Tribes: We need you to lead us 205
Trump, Donald 118
trust 22, 176
Tuckman's model 23-25
Twain, Mark 46
Twilight of the Idols 74
Twister 72, 112, 138, 144

U.S. Navy 23
Uber 142
UFC 98
Union Pacific 101
Ure, Midge 165

values 27, 68, 70, 128-129, 192
Vance, Ashlee 17, 42
Vaynerchuk, Gary 122
videos 187, 189, 190, 191
Virgin Atlantic 188
Virgin Australia 144
visibility 144-145
vision 3, 26
Vistaprint 191
Vitruvius 47
Volkswagen 16

volunteering 163-171
– benefits of 167
– ideas for groups 169
volunteering time off (VTO) 167
vulnerability 78, 79

Wales 149
walks 34, 36
WALL-E 95
Walmart 166
Wang, Xiangpeng 31
wellness program 97, 100
WeWork 142
white paper, structure 138-139
Whitters, Richard 114
Wikipedia 14, 112
Willis, Judy 74
Winer, Dave 120
Winfrey, Oprah 82
winning 194, 197
Wolff, SB 22
Wooder, Bernie 150
Word 139
working from home 175
World Bank 205
World Café 44
Wynhurst Group 66

Y2K 125, *127-128*
Yayici, Emrah 64
yoga 97, 98, 99
YouTube 11, 190

Zapier 69, 70
Zappos 48, 101, 154
Zappos Culture Camp 47
Zendesk 190
Zhang, Wenwen 31
Zoom H6 122

Do you want to deliver culture change but don't know where to start?

Do you want to gain the skills, knowledge and insights that will future-proof your career?

The Culture Fix Community is a one-of-a-kind virtual network where aspirational leaders from around the world work together to enhance their skills and knowledge to build cultures that are productive, competitive, memorable and revered.

Join The Inner Circle and in addition to the Community benefits you will have access to three online programs:

1. Culture Makers Masterclass
2. Project Leadership Academy
3. The EQ Room

Plus monthly webinars, digital resources, keynote videos, live chats with Colin, input into future courses, shared accountability and other exclusive content.

JOIN TODAY!

www.culturefixcommunity.com